SpringerBriefs in Business

More information about this series at http://www.springer.com/series/8860

Cecilia Grieco

Assessing Social Impact of Social Enterprises

Does One Size Really Fit All?

Springer

Cecilia Grieco
Libera Università Maria Ss. Assunta
(LUMSA)
Rome
Italy

ISSN 2191-5482 ISSN 2191-5490 (electronic)
SpringerBriefs in Business
ISBN 978-3-319-15313-1 ISBN 978-3-319-15314-8 (eBook)
DOI 10.1007/978-3-319-15314-8

Library of Congress Control Number: 2015933370

Springer Cham Heidelberg New York Dordrecht London

Springer International Publishing AG Switzerland is part of Springer Science+Business Media
(www.springer.com)

To these five centimetres of pure love,
may you always be proud of your mom

Preface

> The challenge for non-profit scholars is to ensure that research that has relevance for policy, practice, and/or management translates those findings into usable knowledge. In other words, scholars should invest a portion of their writing to address the "so what" question for both research and practice contributions.
>
> —Brenda K. Bushouse and Jessica E. Sowa[1]

I have kept these words in mind while writing this book. The field of study that we analyse as non-profit scholars is a breeding ground for gathering insights and developing new theories to increase our knowledge. But the give-and-take process between theory and practice should be two-way and continuous. I wanted my work to be relevant for practitioners, for whom the issue of assessing the impact of their activities on society is becoming a pressing need.

Several biases have emerged in the discussion of how to measure social impact. Why should organizations spend time and resources measuring what they can see with their own eyes? What benefits can be derived from it? And is it really possible to quantify and/or monetize qualitative data? These are pertinent questions that have often been asked by scholars, but it is difficult to answer them with theoretical contributions. This book is an attempt to find answers to these questions, and to move forward the practice of social impact assessment, most of all within social enterprises.

The reason why I chose to address this topic is the opportunity I have had to study both the theory and practice of the social impact assessment process, which has enabled me to see a wide gap between the former and the latter. Social impact assessment is widely addressed in the literature as an emerging issue and several contributions stress its key role in unlocking new value, especially for social enterprises. The benefits that come from the implementation of this practice have been pointed out by numerous voices. However, it seems that very little of this

---

[1] Bushouse, B. K., & Sowa, J. E. (2012). Producing Knowledge For Practice Assessing NVSQ 2000–2010. *Nonprofit and Voluntary Sector Quarterly*, *41*(3), 497–513.

knowledge is actually perceived and shared by social entrepreneurs in practice. Everyone is now aware of the importance of assessing social impact in improving the activities of organizations, but is everyone aware of the range of tools available for social entrepreneurs in implementing this practice?

This book should be seen as a link that helps readers to "mind the gap" and leads social entrepreneurs into social impact assessment through a better knowledge of models that could support them in driving the process. It addresses entrepreneurs, managers and practitioners who might face this issue in their everyday work, but also scholars and academics, who can further develop and improve the existing body of knowledge through their contributions.

I could not have written this book without the incentives and suggestions of my supervisor, the patience of my colleagues, and the full support of my family and my husband.

A loving thought for you all, and for what is going to come.

Contents

1	**Introduction**		1
	References		4
2	**Conceptualizing Social Entrepreneurship**		5
	2.1	The Origins of the Phenomenon	5
	2.1.1	The Emergence of New Needs	7
	2.1.2	The Limits of the State-Market Binomial	9
	2.1.3	The Crisis of Traditional Business Models	11
	2.1.4	The Social Orientation	12
	2.1.5	The Development of Social Economy	13
	2.2	The Actors of Social Economy	15
	2.3	A Theoretical Approach to Social Entrepreneurship	19
	2.3.1	The Domain of Social Entrepreneurship	20
	2.3.2	Characteristics of Individual Entrepreneurs	22
	2.3.3	The Object of Social Enterprises	25
	2.3.4	The Innovative Approach	26
	2.4	Social Entrepreneurship Across Countries	27
	2.5	The Path for Future Development	31
	References		33
3	**Is Doing Good, Good Enough?**		37
	3.1	From Financial Reporting to Social Accounting	37
	3.2	Developed Theories and Induced Behaviours of Social Awareness	39
	3.2.1	Stakeholder Theory	40
	3.2.2	Shared Value Creation	41
	3.2.3	Triple Bottom Line	42
	3.2.4	Blended Value Proposition	43
	3.3	Defining Social Impact Assessment	44
	3.3.1	The Meaning of Social Impact	44
	3.3.2	The Assessment Process	46

3.3.3 The Meaning of "Social" in Social Impact Assessment: Evolving Perspectives 48
3.4 "The Invisible Heart of Markets": Impact Investing and Social Impact Assessment 50
3.5 Mapping the Practice of Social Impact Assessment in Social Enterprises 54
References. 56

4 How to Drive the Process? 61
4.1 Where to Start? The "Outcome Pathway" to Change 61
4.2 Running the Processes: Steps and Principles. 63
4.3 A Wide Range of Social Impact Assessment Models. 65
4.3.1 An Overview 65
4.3.2 Social Return on Investment. 67
4.3.3 Social Balanced Scorecard 70
4.4 The Rating Game: Monetizing Social Impact 74
4.5 The Need for Classification: A Proposed Taxonomy 75
4.5.1 Simple Social Quantitative. 78
4.5.2 Holistic Complex 80
4.5.3 Qualitative Screening 81
4.5.4 Management 83
4.6 Does One Size Really Fit All? How to Choose the Model 84
References. 89

Annex A: Overview of Existing Models 91

Chapter 1
Introduction

Abstract The purpose of this chapter is to introduce the topic of the analysis and illustrate how the overall book is going to develop. It highlights why the practice of social impact assessment is strategic for social enterprises. As for the key role that social mission plays in this kind of organizations, they have to find a way to measure and monitor the fulfillment of this mission. From this perspective, assessing social impact has both internal and external benefit: it allows to assess resources allocation and to keep stakeholders informed about achieved results. The chapter also explains some of the main barriers that could hamper the implementation of the process. The specificities of social enterprises pose the need for suited models to assess this kind of impact, as financial measurement standards are unsuitable to track social and environmental outcomes. However, a wide range of models exist that can help managers driving the process. Finally the structure of the remaining chapters is outlined.

Keywords Social entrepreneurship · Social mission · Social impact assessment · Models · Self-assessment

In the field of study of social entrepreneurship (SE), much has been said about the process of social impact assessment (SIA) (Richmond et al. 2003; Nicholls 2009; Smith and Stevens 2010). This is because it is increasingly important for organizations that strive to fulfil a social mission to measure the extent to which they are successfully doing so. SE can be seen as a source of solutions to certain illnesses of modern societies (Bacq and Janssen 2011). Similarly to conventional entrepreneurship, it involves the provision of goods and services not as an end in itself, but as an integral part of an intervention to achieve social objectives, thereby contributing to social change. Thus, the defining elements of this kind of organization are no longer the products and services it develops, but its purpose and the ways in which the production is carried out. This means that several types of entities can be considered as social enterprises, including ethical finance, microcredit, fair trade, and more generally all

C. Grieco, *Assessing Social Impact of Social Enterprises*,
SpringerBriefs in Business, DOI 10.1007/978-3-319-15314-8_1

those organizations that produce goods and services with purposes other than their owners' profit, such as the fight against poverty and malnutrition (Yunus 2008).

Univocally defining social enterprises is a hard job. They can widely differ from several perspectives (legal form, sector of activity, profit management), but they all share the common feature of striving for the achievement of a social mission. The key role of solving social issues makes the need to assess the generated impact highly important for these organizations. The importance of SIA has been highlighted both from academic and practitioner perspectives, and has been further underlined by international organizations. The OECD (2010), for example, among the preliminary recommendations drawn up for the improvement of SE and social innovation, remarked on the need to properly evaluate the impact of social entrepreneurs in selected areas.

All organizations face the challenge of how to assess performance beyond current financial metrics, but this is becoming a particular concern for social enterprises. As they use business methods to achieve social goals, they are normally accountable to a complex range of stakeholders, and yet are often low to medium in terms of organizational capacity (Meadows and Pike 2010). They therefore feel this challenge especially strongly (Grimes 2010).

The value of this process is twofold. First, it can be used as an internal tool to assist the process of resources allocation and support social entrepreneurs in managing the organization. Second, it is a reporting tool that can be used to keep stakeholders updated on the objectives that the organization is achieving. This last point is particularly important, as it refers to funders who might want to be reassured of the worthiness of their investments. This is also linked to the importance of SIA in its connection with the disbursement of funds to solve social issues. Phenomena such as the spread of impact investing tools, witnessing the recent developments in new vehicles and metrics to apply investment models to solve social problems, opens room for shared practice to ensure the achievement of planned solutions.

However, the difficulties in identifying qualitative and quantitative metrics for reporting information make the assessment of social impact problematic. To address this complexity, many different models have been developed by different entities, aimed at providing guidelines and indicators for the implementation of the process. This ongoing proliferation of models is due to the fact that organizations differ in size, capacity, activities and focus, and consequently there is no single model that is suitable for all of them.

The need for creating new tools lies in the unsuitability of traditional financial accounting, which does not completely track the benefits created by social entrepreneurs (Epstein and Buhovac 2014). Intangible and non-monetized items are normally not included in financial reports (Richmond et al. 2003); while despite the earned revenues, SEs have a social mission, and the inclusion in the financial statements of the social benefits they create is significant as it provides a more complete view of their overall performance (Austin et al. 2006).

The wide range of existing models is of course a strength for social entrepreneurs who want to implement a SIA process, but it can on the other hand generate confusion, making the choice of which one to adopt more difficult. The underlying belief from which this work begins is that social enterprises have become a real propelling engine for economic recovery in the current scenario, where the traditional binomial of state and market is no longer enough to solve the emerging social issues and meet the new needs of societies. From this perspective, several efforts have been made to foster the development of SE, and the benefits associated with SIA can of course support its growth. Unfortunately, despite the growing interest from both academia and practitioners, the empirical approach to this process is still confused and not well-regulated. Several barriers hamper SIA diffusion, with negative consequences also for the implementation of impact investing tools that require some shared forms of measuring social impact to be effectively adopted. The main purpose is to foster a better knowledge of SIA models, and provide entrepreneurs with some indication of how to find the one that could best fit their needs.

The remainder of this book is structured as follows. Chapter 2 provides an overview of the concept of SE, illustrating its origins and development within the whole phenomenon of social economy. Particular attention is paid to providing an overall vision of the features of this complex concept and illustrating those elements that are mostly debated in the attempts to draft a generally accepted definition. Data is included about how the landscape of social enterprises is shaped across countries.

Chapter 3 introduces the topic of SIA, highlighting its meaning and implications. Along with a detailed definition of what social impact actually means and what role the measurement process can have, the benefits that could come from this practice are illustrated, as well as the main barriers that could hamper its implementation. There is a specific focus on impact investing, which has emerged in several countries that have witnessed the trend of using investment models to solve social needs. The pivotal role of SIA in relation to these tools is explained in this chapter.

Finally, Chap. 4 presents an in-depth analysis of the process of SIA in its principles and main steps, focusing on existing models. The Social Return On Investment (SROI) and the Social Balanced Scorecard (SBSC) are described, illustrating the principles on which they were developed and the indicators they use to guide the assessment process. A taxonomy is then proposed to offer an attempt at classification that can help social entrepreneurs to address the great number of models available, followed by a description of the main features of four groups of SIA models. The chapter ends with a self-assessment on models aimed at guiding social entrepreneurs in selecting the group of models that best meets the specific needs of their organizations.

Annex 1 includes the description of 75 SIA models. A brief table for each one presents information about the promoter, the purpose of the model and its main contents.

References

Austin, J., Stevenson, H., & Wei-Skillern, J. (2006). Social and commercial entrepreneurship: Same, different, or both? *Entrepreneurship theory and practice, 30*(1), 1–22.

Bacq, S., & Janssen, F. (2011). The multiple faces of social entrepreneurship: A review of definitional issues based on geographical and thematic criteria. *Entrepreneurship and Regional Development, 23*(5–6), 373–403.

Epstein, M. J., & Buhovac, A. R. (2014). *Making sustainability work: Best practices in managing and measuring corporate social, environmental, and economic impacts.* Sheffield: Berrett-Koehler Publishers.

Grimes, M. (2010). Strategic sense making within funding relationships: The effects of performance measurement on organizational identity in the social sector. *Entrepreneurship Theory and Practice, 34*(4), 763–783.

Meadows, M., & Pike, M. (2010). Performance management for social enterprises. *Systemic Practice and Action Research, 23*(2), 127–141.

Nicholls, A. (2009). We do good things, don't we?: Blended value accounting in social entrepreneurship. *Accounting Organizations and Society, 34*, 755–769.

OECD. (2010). SMEs, entrepreneurship and innovation. http://www.oecd.org/document/16/0,3746,en_2649_33956792_44938128_1_1_1_1,00.html.

Richmond, B. J., Mook, L., & Quarter, J. (2003). Social accounting for non profits: Two models. *Non-profit Management and Leadership, 13*(4), 308–324.

Smith, B. R., & Stevens, C. E. (2010). Different types of social entrepreneurship: The role of geography and embeddedness on the measurement and scaling of social value. *Entrepreneurship and Regional Development, 22*(6), 575–598.

Yunus, M. (2008). *A world without poverty: Social business and the future of capitalism.* New York, USA: Public Affairs.

Chapter 2
Conceptualizing Social Entrepreneurship

Where We Are and How to Move Forward

Abstract The purpose of this chapter is to outline the concept of social entrepreneurship, describing its origins within the whole phenomenon of social economy. Particular attention is paid to providing an overall vision of the features of this complex concept, and illustrating those elements that are mostly debated in the attempts to draft a generally accepted definition. The differences emerging across countries concerning the concept of social entrepreneurship will also be touched upon. This chapter provides an overview of what social enterprises are and the reason why assessing social impact is highly beneficial for them.

Keywords Social entrepreneurship · Social economy · Non-profit organization · Social mission · Entrepreneur

2.1 The Origins of the Phenomenon

The concept of social entrepreneurship (SE) is an innovative field of research that has recently been recognized as a dominant discourse within the field of studies on entrepreneurship. Its growing importance and the associated academic and managerial interest are evident in the increasing number of publications aimed at better investigating this concept.

Since the late 1990s, a worldwide and unprecedented surge in interest in the topic has been fostered by significant changes in the political, economic and environmental scenarios. These changes have led policy-makers, conscious citizens and disadvantaged communities to turn to private entrepreneurs for innovative and sustainable solutions that address poverty and related problems as the root causes of inequality and the uneven distribution of the world's wealth (Nicholls 2006; Shaw et al. 2013).

These alternative approaches to sustainable economic development have drawn the attention of academic researchers who are particularly interested in investigating the manifestation of entrepreneurial behaviour and practices within the context of social rather than personal gain. While, indeed, entrepreneurial phenomena aimed at

C. Grieco, *Assessing Social Impact of Social Enterprises*,
SpringerBriefs in Business, DOI 10.1007/978-3-319-15314-8_2

economic development have received a great amount of scholarly attention, entrepreneurship as a process to foster social progress has only in the last decades particularly attracted the interest of researchers.

Research on SE has clearly drawn on and benefited from previous work on entrepreneurship. Approaches and constructs stemming from research on entrepreneurship in the business sector shaped the first attempts to conceptualize the phenomenon of SE (*ibid*). The concept of entrepreneurship refers to the identification, evaluation and exploitation of opportunities to bring new products or services into existence as new outputs to be sold at prices higher than their cost of production (Eckhardt and Shane 2003). This definition implies that the fundamental mission of entrepreneurial activities involves profit generation and entrepreneurs' personal wealth. Analogously, SE refers to the identification, evaluation and exploitation of opportunities, and involves profit generation just as entrepreneurial activities do; this profit helps entrepreneurs to build personal wealth. However, the opportunities identified by social entrepreneurs result in social value as opposed to personal or shareholder wealth. The notion of opportunity recognition is at the heart of entrepreneurship, both in its traditional and social meaning; however, SE opportunities are different from their traditional counterpart (Austin et al. 2006). Opportunities recognized by social entrepreneurs arise from social problems and involve the attempt to create social value. Social value has little to do with profits as it concerns the fulfilment of basic and long-standing needs such as providing food, water, shelter, education, and medical services (Certo and Miller 2008).

The fusion of the entrepreneurial root and the social component led to the development of social enterprises as organizations in which economic activity is leveraged to pursue a social objective and implement a social change. SE involves the provision of goods and services, analogously to conventional entrepreneurship. However this is not an end in itself, but a means to achieve social objectives, thus contributing to social change. The focus on economic activity is important to differentiate SE from pure forms of social movements as well as from charitable and philanthropic initiatives. Yet, the transformative social ambition distinguishes SE from entrepreneurship with a conscience and other forms of doing good such as CSR or corporate philanthropy. Social entrepreneurs do not merely aim to make money without harming their environment; rather, the achievement of the social mission that they pursue is their primary objective. In this view, SE necessarily involves the entrepreneurial perspective as a form of income-generating venture aimed at social benefits instead of pure profit (Peredo and McLean 2006; Mair et al. 2012).

The relation between profit-seeking and social purpose is at the root of the development of the wider concept of social economy, in which the phenomenon of SE falls. Despite the recent attention, this is not an entirely new perspective. For at least the past century, scholars and business practitioners from a wide range of disciplinary backgrounds have deliberated over whether business should influence or merely reflect social norms and expectations. Among them, Porter and Kramer (2006, 2011) highlighted the mutual dependence between corporations and society, implying that both business decisions and social policies must follow the principle of creating shared value resulting in choices benefiting both sides.

Nevertheless, there are some elements that make current studies different from previous efforts. First, the language used is new and implies a blurring of the boundaries between the non-profit and for-profit sectors and the emergence of hybrid organizations mixing elements of both. This helps to broaden the playing field and allows social enterprises to look for the most effective methods of serving their social mission. Second, in comparison with the past, the number and range of social actors behaving entrepreneurially is far larger than at any other point in history (Bornstein 2004). Thirdly, and even more significantly, the impact that social entrepreneurs are aiming to achieve is also far more ambitious than ever before, and they are able to bring about systemic changes by influencing social behaviour on a global scale (Nicholls 2005). These features make this field of study ever more attractive and different enough to warrant its own body of theory (Weerawardena and Mort 2006; Murphy and Coombes 2009).

The emergence of the social economy has been due to a convergence of elements inside and outside organizations that created the basis for the definition and the gradual growth of these kinds of entities. Figure 2.1 shows these identified elements. In the following sections each of these trends will be described in light of its role as a favourable variable in the development of social economy and social enterprises.

2.1.1 The Emergence of New Needs

In the current economy trends such as globalization, low rates of economic growth, and the increasing complexity of society have radically changed the model of development. These trends have resulted in the emergence of new needs and growing demand for new services. Demographic and economic shifts over the past few decades have brought about significant changes in the needs of the population. Increasing life expectancy, the entrance of women into the workforce, migratory flows, and the emergence of a more knowledge-based economy are just some examples of the changes we have seen. These developments have at the same time

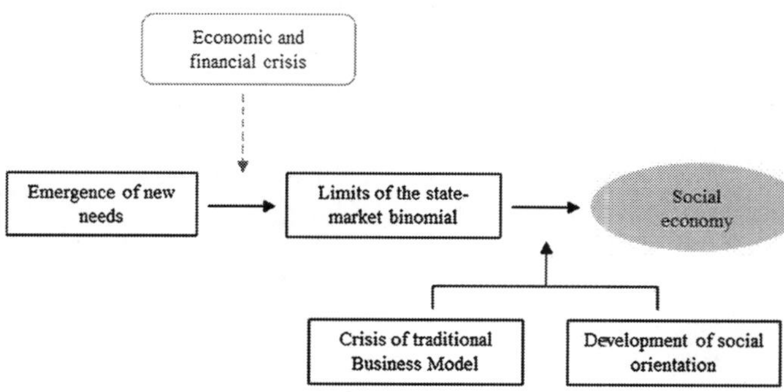

Fig. 2.1 Macro-trends leading to social economy

been the source of new problems that have required new solutions: improved ways to care for the elderly; child care as a major new area of intervention; new policy tools to ensure the economic and social integration of migrants; a continuous diversification and improvement of the education system. In addition, society needs to find appropriate responses to climate change and dwindling natural resources (Borzaga et al. 2014). Thus, the emergence of new needs and the increasing differentiation of existing ones have made demands by citizens more wide-ranging and complex.

Contrary to widely held beliefs, unfulfilled basic needs are present not only in developing countries, and this modern state of affairs forces us to look at developed countries from a different perspective. An example is the worrying data on growing poverty that European countries are currently facing.

Box 2.1: New poverty in European countries
One of the five headline targets of the Europe 2020 Headline indicators is indeed the reduction of poverty, by lifting at least 20 million people out of the risk of poverty by 2020. According to Eurostat (2013), within the Euro28 area there are more than 120 million (24.8 %) people at risk of poverty or social exclusion. Considerable variations are evident among the member states, though the overall rate slightly increased between 2011 and 2012 (0.5 % points). Some unexpected trends have emerged, such as the fact that children are more at risk of poverty than elderly people in several countries. The main factors determining child poverty are the employment situation of their parents, which is linked to their level of education; the household in which they live; and the effectiveness of government intervention. Also, the number of children with migrant parents is growing: a vulnerable group that deserves particular attention. Conversely, the elderly face a lower risk of poverty or social exclusion than the overall Euro28 population.

Individuals considered at risk of poverty or social exclusion are identified as those living below the poverty threshold, severely materially deprived, or living in households with very low work intensity (defined as the ratio between the number of months that household members of working age worked during the income reference year, and the total number of months that could theoretically have been worked by the same household members). Those living in households with very low work intensity comprise 10.3 % of the population, while people whose disposable income is below their national at-risk-of-poverty threshold comprise 17 %. Finally, material deprivation—the condition of being severely affected by a lack of resources—affects 9.9 % of the population. The greatest variation from 2011 to 2012 concerns the ability of the population to face unexpected expenses (calculated as 1/12 of the poverty threshold). In 2012, 40.2 % of the population reported difficulties with covering the cost of their own resources, representing an increase of 2.1 percentage points compared with 2011.

What this data shows is that poverty rates are quite high, and not only in developing countries. Moreover, in light of the new needs of the population, the concept of poverty is now acquiring new and different meanings. The term "new poverty" has indeed been coined, referring not only to people's economic conditions but also to the wider conditions of uncertainty and instability in which people often live. From this new perspective the concept of poverty reflects the fragility of relations, job insecurity, and feelings of inadequacy in a system where competitiveness and productivity are the dominant elements. All this comes from the demographic and social changes within societies, and includes ever more categories (e.g. elderly living alone, young couples, single parents, the unemployed).

It is possible to say that today the concept of poverty is giving way to that of social exclusion, which concerns the impossibility of, inability to, or discrimination against participating in those activities that determine for an individual their belonging to a certain community or social group. The "excluded" are thus those who have no access to social life in terms of employment, education and training, or the possibility of creating a family. The basic difference is that this issue is no longer only about money and income; rather, the focus has shifted to the relational aspects of exclusion.

An emerging need is that of social cohesion, where stable social ties are built through economic, social, cultural, political and civil institutions. Social cohesion in very often the object of the activities of social enterprises. In this sense their goal is to eradicate barriers to social cohesion such as a lack of material and intangible means, those cognitive or physical elements that hamper people from having social ties, and the lack of access to employment, welfare benefits, and social and healthcare services. The concept of social exclusion is strongly linked to the quality of interpersonal relationships, and is indeed more dynamic and operative than economic poverty (Fondazione 2007).

These tendencies have made advanced economies into breeding grounds for the emergence of new kinds of businesses whose services are specifically tailored to addressing the emerging needs. In this sense, SE refers to a process of catering to locally existing basic needs that are not addressed by traditional organizations. Social enterprises are indeed characterized by the innovative approach with which they address social issues and find solutions to problematic situations. Depending on the need addressed, the process can involve the provision of goods or services and/or the creation of missing institutions, or the reshaping of inadequate ones. However, SE's main objective is to change or modify the social and/or economic arrangements that have created the situation of failure to satisfy basic needs.

2.1.2 The Limits of the State-Market Binomial

The current scenario is characterized by unique and unparalleled challenges at global as well as national and local levels, and requires new strategies and tools to successfully address these challenges. This cannot be accomplished by the market or the state on their own: the economic, social and political institutions that are designed to cater to the basic needs and rights of individuals in society can fail to serve large segments of the population. From the state perspective, the need for new approaches also arises in the presence of the systematic retreat of government from the provision of public goods in the face of new political ideologies that stress citizens' self-sufficiency and give primacy to market-driven models of welfare (Nicholls 2006). The economic crisis has also played a crucial role, as it has increased the inability of governments to meet the social needs of their constituencies (Pless 2012). From the market perspective, several industries have been severely penalized by the economic crisis, and the profit-seeking purpose they fulfil is often threatened by consumers' spending reductions. Moreover, companies are strictly evaluated by consumers according to their social perspective (see Sect. 2.1.4), and purchasing behaviour is increasingly used as a means to reward or punish companies' choices.

Economic globalization offers several opportunities to improve living conditions, but the simultaneous desire for continuous restructuring and change requires renewed and completely new approaches aimed at promoting sustainable economic and social development, to recover the economy and diffuse the benefits. Innovation is indeed one of the key elements underpinning economic growth, as it allows the development of new solutions to the current challenges of society. The creation of innovative business ventures can play a critical role in fostering the innovation process, because of their ability to recognize and exploit the commercial opportunities coming from technological and competitive and market changes (OECD 2010).

This is the reason why the emergence of initiatives aimed at changing the world (Bornstein 2004) have become even more inspiring. The examples of entrepreneurs who look for and design solutions for unmet social needs, and whose primary intention is to help others, are a source of hope in markets where traditional forms of capitalism are concerned with rebuilding their own reputation and legitimacy (Pless 2012). SE arises to tackle social challenges and to respond to them when the market and the public sector do not. This concept is well explained by Santos (2012), who points out the specificities of SE as opposed to traditional forms of entrepreneurship, referring to the dichotomy of value creation and value capture. The former refers to the creation of a strong and important impact for society in general, while the latter concerns the appropriation of a substantial portion of the value created with the aim of making a profit. As the author states, neither profit-oriented companies nor governments, due to a lack of resources, will systematically engage in areas and activities perceived as having a high potential for value creation but little potential for value capture (such as eradicating diseases or malnutrition in developing countries). These situations remain the domain of social entrepreneurs. Social enterprises have structural features that allow them to fill the gaps of the other parties. On the one hand, their striving for a social mission leads them to accomplish only goals that could benefit society as a whole, rather than seeking to earn profit regardless of its social impact; while on the other hand, as they fund their growth with their profits, they keep themselves independent from funders' requirements that could constrain them (e.g. the desire for venture capitalists to earn back their investments more quickly, a foundation's requirement to have social goals reached in a specific way, or government's decreased funding in the face of budget cuts) (Massetti 2008).

2.1.3 The Crisis of Traditional Business Models

The ongoing crisis has accelerated the need for rethinking the respective roles of the market, the state, the third sector and the individual, and helped identify some of the values and directions in which development should move. In this context, the call for new forms of organizations that move away from the capitalist system, and bring into question the logic underlying the traditional business models, is strongly felt. The emerging need is for a "more sophisticated form of capitalism" that is in some way connected with social purpose. Social purpose is no longer just the responsibility of non-profit organizations or charity activities; rather, it has to be understood as something that emerges from the combination of economic activities and social mission, and blurs the boundaries between traditionally different kinds of enterprises, developing new ways of engaging with society (Porter and Kramer 2006).

These principles have been the basis for the development of new industries in which the traditional way of doing business is substantially redrafted. Among the main examples, microfinance is of course worth mentioning. This concept refers to the pioneering idea of Nobel Prize winner Muhammad Yunus of creating ways to grant funds to those who are typically not served by commercial banks. Formal financial institutions are indeed not designed to help people who do not already have financial assets. This is mostly because large loans allow banks to make more money compared to small loans, and the same goes for savings accounts. In this way poor people are omitted from traditional financial services and have to adopt informal savings mechanisms, with the serious limitations that they imply.

Microfinance consists of supplying loans, savings and other basic financial services to the poor. Its core idea is that low-income individuals are capable of lifting themselves out of poverty if given access to financial services. Although credit unions and lending cooperatives have been around for years, the groundbreaking example of modern microfinance is the Grameen Bank, a microfinance organization and community development bank founded in Bangladesh by Muhammad Yunus in 1983. The Grameen Bank serves 5.8 million borrowers, 96 % of whom are women, representing as many families. The borrowers own the bank, which lends over half a billion dollars a year in loans averaging USD $120, without any collateral or legal instruments. The bank lends for income-generating purposes, for housing, and for the higher education of the children of the borrowers; it also lends to beggars without interest. Its deposit base is larger than the loans outstanding (Yunus 2003). It is important to note that the bank is not in the red: 98 % of loans are repaid. Moreover, the bank collects deposits, provides other services, and manages several economic activities aimed at fostering development.

These kinds of innovative businesses are those that best meet the current situation that has emerged. Social enterprises have new ways of organizing work through the involvement of different partners and several categories of actors: salaried workers, volunteers, users, support organizations and local public authorities are often partners in the same project. Not only does this revolutionize the production process; it also transforms the way in which the activity is organized, which in some cases is a kind of joint construction of supply and demand where providers and users cooperate in the organization and management of certain proximity services (Defourny and Nyssens 2013).

2.1.4 The Social Orientation

At the beginning of the 20th century, the main problem for entrepreneurs was how to produce. In this phase their focus was on production and required technical equipment, and firms were indeed defined as *production-oriented*. The years after World War II were the basis for the subsequent economic boom, with the rise and development of new firms in every sector. At that point firms that wanted to survive and achieve success became *market-oriented*, as they could not ignore the market and meet its needs in a careful and precise way. Afterward, the practices of adopting proactive behaviour, paying attention to trends, and changing place to be able to anticipate and in some ways address those needs, became an urge. Together with the growing difficulty in acquiring customers' spending capacity, this aspect was an imperative that required the *marketing-oriented* adaptation of firms' strategies and philosophies. During the 1960s and the early 1970s the slow industrialization together with the impact that it had on environment, the economic crisis and the associated high social tensions, the growing dynamicity, and the sudden and significant changes that affected environmental contests, led firms to a highly important realization: they could not concentrate only on the market and customers, but they also had to address the environment in its general sense and create relationships of trust with all the stakeholders. This rediscovery of the ethical aspects of production, and a parallel pressure on firms to adopt socially responsible behaviours, led to the *social orientation* that is currently predominant. Also, the development of communication technologies and the consequent increased access to information helped people to become aware of social issues and of the ability of their behaviour as consumers to apply pressure to private enterprises for the adoption of more responsible business practices.

The orientation towards social issues occurs mainly along three dimensions (Euricse 2013). The first one concerns the behaviour of the individual. People have become more aware of the impact that their consumer behaviour can have on the social outcomes they care about. This consumer empowerment involves easily acquiring information on how the goods one buys are produced, and organizing collective action in order to put pressure on producers and regulators. The rise of so-called responsible consumption is based on the importance of social and environmental implications of production as key elements to drive purchasing behaviours. As a result, it is no longer a matter of price and quality; rather, consumers tend to reward products that meet ethical standards or have an impact on local development.

A second dimension concerns savings and finance as another side of socially responsible consumer behaviour that is not limited to the purchase of goods and services, but extends to interest in where to invest money and what is being done with savings. The internet has engendered the development of many forms of social investment, and allows people to directly support the projects or organizations of their choice.[1] This trend is reflected in the whole financial service sector, where the recent development of new vehicles and metrics to evaluate investment opportunities based on social and environmental impact in addition to financial returns is evidence of the efforts made in applying investment models to solve social needs.

Finally, the third dimension concerns corporate behaviour and the strengthening of CSR as a voluntary inclusion of ethical standards within the practices of conventional businesses that do not have an explicit social mission. Social attention within corporate strategies can take on different forms that range from pure philanthropy, where a business donates part of its profits; directly or through foundations, to other organizations that address social goals; to double and triple bottom line approaches, where the goal is to maximize social and environmental outcomes along with shareholder return. As the social orientation of consumers has grown in relation to these three perspectives, a shift is occurring from CSR to more structured forms of shared value creation (Porter and Kramer 2006), where the engagement with society is deeper as it becomes the core mission of the organizations.

2.1.5 The Development of Social Economy

The variables described above have played a significant role in determining the appropriate context in which the phenomenon of social economy has been born. Social economy is described as an entrepreneurial, not-for-profit sector that seeks to enhance the social, economic and environmental conditions of communities (Restakis 2006). The term is often confused with social market economy. While similar in name, they refer to two quite different political and economic concepts. Social economy is used to define a specific part of the economy that works alongside the market and the state (see Fig. 2.2): a set of organizations that primarily pursue social aims and are characterized by participative governance systems.

---

[1] An important example in recent years is the rise of crowdfunding as a way of directly mobilizing financial resources for the most disparate ventures. The term refers to the practice of funding a project or venture by raising many small amounts of money from a large number of people, typically via the internet.

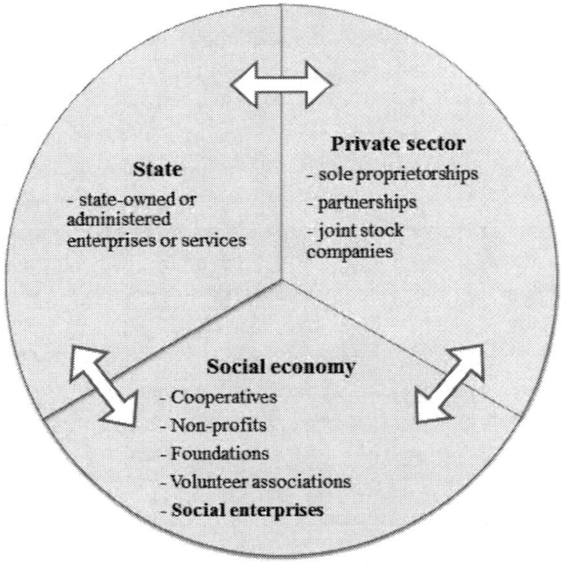

Fig. 2.2 The place of social economy [It is important to note that while the three areas are certainly distinct and the institutions within them operate on different economic principles, they are not hermetically sealed off from each other. There are several transfers and borrowings from one to the other and certain organizations operate at the boundaries of these distinctions. Universities might be placed at the borders of the public and private sectors. So might public/private partnerships. And some non-profit/private partnerships could be placed at the borders of the social economy and the private sector (Restakis 2006)]. Adapted by Restakis (2006)

The term "social market economy" instead refers to a political-economic model created after World War II to harmonize the principle of social security by giving the state an active role in promoting both market competition and balanced social development. Two main pillars of state action represent the base of the social market economy: on the one hand, competition has to be enforced to keep prices stable and generate growth and innovation; while on the other, social policy measures must foresee negative outcomes and ensure social protection. These principles, at first strongly embedded across Europe, were gradually changed by new actors and behaviours that have brought about a richer and more complex economic ecosystem, in which the state can no longer be seen as the only possible provider of social services.

In its historical roots, social economy is linked to popular associations and cooperatives whose systems of values and principles of conduct are reflected in the modern meaning of the concept. This is because these forms are interlinked expressions of a single impulse: the response of the most vulnerable and defenceless social groups, through self-help organizations, to the new living conditions created by the development of industrial society in the 18th and 19th centuries (Castellano 2003). Although charity and mutual assistance organizations had a considerable growth throughout the Middle Ages, working classes' initiatives during the 19th century gave to popular associations, cooperatives and mutual societies an extraordinary impetus (Chaves and Monzón 2012).

2.2 The Actors of Social Economy

Organizations falling within the concept of social economy are animated by the principle of reciprocity for the pursuit of mutual economic or social goals, often through the social control of capital. The overall aim of their activities does not emphasize the pursuit of profit and its distribution to the owners as an ultimate goal. Instead, the main objectives for which these organizations strive include the provision of goods and services to their members or community and the pursuit of general interest goals. Fulfilling this kind of purpose means, for instance, that these organizations tend to preserve employment and quality of service to their members and customers even at the cost of reducing their margin of profit. Another feature shared by many social economy organizations is their ownership structure. In these organizations indeed ownership rights are assigned to stakeholders other than investors (e.g. workers, customers, volunteers), and their involvement and participation are highly valued. Voluntary work is another element that characterizes social economy organizations, as well as democratic decision-making processes, whereby decisions concerning the organization are voted upon by all of its members. Included organizations share the aforementioned features, but can be notably different among each other and, within the same category, also vary considerably from one country to another.

Generally it is possible to identify four groups of social economy organizations. Social cooperatives are member-owned organizations that abide by the principles of democracy and solidarity and are focused on social value creation. Their main aim is providing answers to the needs of the community or some vulnerable group in the community. Social cooperatives first appeared in 1991, when the Italian parliament adopted a law that established them as member-owned organizations operating with the purpose of creating social value for communities (Carini and Costa 2013). According to this law, social cooperatives can be involved in either caring or training activities. Caring activities (type A) refer to social, healthcare, educational and cultural services, as well as nurseries and initiatives aimed at environmental protection. Training activities (type B) involve all those initiatives that aim to provide job-placement services for disadvantaged people (Thomas 2004).

A second group are mutual societies, or mutuals, which are autonomous associations of persons united voluntarily for the primary purpose of satisfying their common needs in the insurance, providence, health and banking sectors, and whose activities are subject to competition (Chaves and Monzón 2012). Unlike cooperatives, whose capital is represented by shares, mutual funds are owned and managed jointly and indivisibly. To join the mutual society, future members have to pay for the services provided without buying a share in the capital or paying membership costs.

A third type is the association, which is a lasting organization for a particular purpose that can be cultural as well as recreational, social or economic in nature, which in the end seeks to meet the general interests of society. Usually, an association provides services to its members, to other people (often specific categories of people, e.g. Save the Children), or to the community as a whole (e.g. Greenpeace). Associations can be formal, with rules, by-laws and membership requirements, or they can be an informal collection of people without a set structure.

Finally, foundations are organizations that involve the use of an endowment or systematic fundraising activities, and are managed by legal entities created to accomplish specific goals for the benefit of a specific group of people or of the community as a whole. The use of the endowment is thus linked to the achievement of the statutory purposes. These organizations are above all committed to promoting social, religious and educational activities according to the funder's will. The way in which the endowment is used distinguishes operating foundations from grant-making foundations. The former are equipped with one or more structures (e.g. care homes, libraries, research centres) aimed at the fulfilment of their mission, providing goods and services of general interest, usually working in the fields of the arts, culture, social care and health. In the latter case no activities are carried out by the foundations; rather, they dispense grants and contributions to other entities, generally non-profit organizations, who with the received resources can provide goods and services to society. Examples of this category are corporate foundations, private entities that derive their funds primarily from the contributions of a profit-making business.

In 2012, the European Economic and Social Committee tried to map the social economy phenomenon across European countries, considering the aforementioned groups. Table 2.1 summarizes what emerged from the survey, illustrating the extent of the phenomenon.

What is evidenced by this data is a predominance of associations and foundations compared to the other analysed categories. The countries with the most entities are the United Kingdom (870,000) and Germany (505,984). Italy is the country with the highest number of cooperatives (71,578), followed by France and (24,870) and Poland (8,823). The lowest occurrence is in Luxembourg (56), Malta (57) and Latvia (74), in keeping with the smaller dimensions of these countries. As for mutual organizations, the number of entities is almost always less than 100, with some exceptions like France (6,743), Romania (897), Germany (328), the Netherlands (124) and Finland (106).

The aforementioned groups are just a way to simplify the variegated landscape of organizations that fall within the social economy. Actually social economy organizations can often adopt a mixture of organizational forms. They can be, for example, voluntary associations that control a foundation, or foundations that control associations or other organizations. Sometimes social economy organizations can even adopt enterprise forms that typically belong to the for-profit sector.

According to the European Economic and Social Committee, social economy organizations fall into two major sub-sectors: (a) the market or business sub-sector, and (b) the non-market producer sub-sector. Some features are shared by both

Table 2.1 The social economy in Europe. Adapted by Chaves and Monzón (2012)

	Cooperatives and other similar accepted forms	Mutual companies and other similar accepted forms	Associations, foundations and other similar accepted forms
Austria	1860 enterprises	59 entities	116,556 entities
	61,999 jobs	1416 jobs	170,113 jobs
	3,015,614 members		4,670,000 volunteers
Belgium	166 enterprises	26 enterprises	18,461 entities
	13,547 jobs	11,974 jobs	437,020 jobs
	2,670,000 members		
Bulgaria	2,016 enterprises	11 entities	22,315 entities
	41,300 jobs	12,525 members	80,000 jobs
	425,000 members		1,459,000 members
Cyprus	620 enterprises	n.a.	3516 entities
	5067 jobs		
	1,275,993 members		
Czech Republic	3085 enterprises	7 entities	98,693 entities
	58,178 jobs	5679 jobs	96,229 jobs
	754,697 members		
Denmark	523 enterprises	53 entities	12,877 entities
	70,757 jobs	4072 jobs	120,657 jobs
	1,840,803 members		
Estonia	1604 enterprises	n.a.	32,000 entities
	9850 jobs		28,000 jobs
	410,000 members		
Finland	4,384 enterprises	106 entities	130,000 entities
	94,100 jobs	8,500 jobs	84,600 jobs
	3,865,400 members		
France	24,870 enterprises	6,743 entities	160,844 entities
	320,822 jobs	128,710 jobs	1,869,012 jobs
	24,000,000 members	20,000,000 members	14,000,000 volunteers
Germany	7,415 enterprises	328 entities	505,984 entities
	830,258 jobs	86,497 jobs	1,541,829 jobs
	20,509,973 members		3,000,000 volunteers
Greece	7197 enterprises	11 entities	50,600 entities
	14,983 jobs	1140 jobs	101,000 jobs
	1,052,785 members	180,000 members	1,500,000 members
Hungary	2769 entities	13 entities	58,242 entities
	85,682 jobs	6,676 jobs	85,852 jobs
	547,000 members		
Ireland	509 enterprises	100 entities	25,000 entities
	43,328 jobs	650 jobs	54,757 jobs
	152,000 members		1,570,408 volunteers

(continued)

Table 2.1 (continued)

	Cooperatives and other similar accepted forms	Mutual companies and other similar accepted forms	Associations, foundations and other similar accepted forms
Italy	71,578 enterprises	n.a.	26,121 entities
	1,128,381 jobs		1,099,629 jobs
	12,293,202 members		899,309 volunteers
Latvia	74 enterprises	n.a.	n.a.
	440 jobs		
	17,330 members		
Lithuania	490 enterprises	n.a.	22,000 entities
	8971 jobs		
	221,858 members		
Luxembourg	56 enterprises	n.a.	664 entities
	1,933 jobs		14,181 jobs
	5203 members		
Malta	57 enterprises	n.a.	693 members
	250 jobs		1427 jobs
	5663 members		7,058 volunteers
The Netherlands	677 enterprises	124 entities	60,000 entities
	184,053 jobs	2860 jobs	699,121 jobs
	3,249,000 members		
Poland	8823 enterprises	22 entities	86,100 entities
	400,000 jobs	2800 jobs	190,000 jobs
	8,000,000 members		
Portugal	2390 enterprises	95 entities	45,543 entities
	51,391 jobs	5,500 jobs	194,207 jobs
	1,353,107 members	1,100,000 members	
Romania	1,747 enterprises	897 entities	23,100 entities
	34,373 jobs	18,999 jobs	109,982 jobs
	809,170 members		
Slovakia	382 enterprises	10 entities	26,210 entities
	26,090 jobs	2158 jobs	16,658 jobs
	570,845 members	57,000 members	118,623 volunteers
Slovenia	77 enterprises	3 entities	21,000 entities
	3428 jobs	476 jobs	3190 jobs
	16,903 members		
United Kingdom	5,450 enterprises	105 enterprises	870,000 entities
	236,000 jobs	50,000 jobs	1,347,000 jobs
	12,800,000 members		10,600,000 volunteers

Data from Euricse, Legacoop and Confcooperative, data on cooperatives and mutual societies only for those affiliated with these confederations (Chaves and Monzón 2012) sectors: they are private organizations, formally organized; they have autonomy of decision and freedom of membership, and are democratic. Also, any distribution of profits is not proportional to the capital or the fees contributed by the members, because even if they work *with* capital they do not work *for* capital but for the achievement of social change. The difference among the sectors lies in the market orientation of first sector, as they are market producers and their output is mainly intended for sale on the market at economically significant prices. In this context social enterprises are a clear example of a hybrid of market and non-market, with a wide diversity of resources (revenue from the market, public subsidies and voluntary work) and of agents within the organization (members, employees, volunteers, companies and public bodies).

Both within and alongside the universe of social economy organizations, social enterprises have emerged in recent years as a new and very significant worldwide phenomenon. Despite the lack of a universal definition, the term is increasingly used to identify a different way of doing business, which occurs when enterprises are created specifically to pursue social goals. What distinguishes social enterprises from traditional social economy organizations is the fact that a substantial proportion of their income should come through trading, rather than being dependent on grants or donations. A benchmark sometimes used for a social enterprise is that at least 50 % of its turnover is earned income, although opinions vary on what the best threshold would be. The underlying principle is that social enterprises have a primary social purpose, and the majority of any profit is reinvested or otherwise used to achieve the social mission of the enterprise.

2.3 A Theoretical Approach to Social Entrepreneurship

Although the concept of SE is gaining popularity among academics, what emerges from a literature analysis is a lack of consensus about what SE really is; in spite of the great number of publications aimed at gaining a better understanding of this phenomenon, it still means "different things to different people" (Dees 1998, p. 1). The literature on this topic has grown in significance over the last two decades. Kraus et al. (2013) developed an exploratory citation analysis of research on SE and the results show that, particularly in 2009 and 2010, the number of empirical research articles published rose significantly.

Of course SE is a complex phenomenon, and definitions are hardly able to capture the whole picture. Problems with univocally defining the concept also depend on the fact that these entities vary greatly according to the geographical context, and that countries recognize SE differently. At any rate, it is essential to begin by being clear about what SE is, and this is a purpose that has been widely pursued. The fact that scholars have not yet reached a general definition is partly due to the newness of the topic, as well as to the difficulty of drawing demarcation lines between SE and other fields such as commercial entrepreneurship and business management.

Fig. 2.3 Grouping definitions of SE

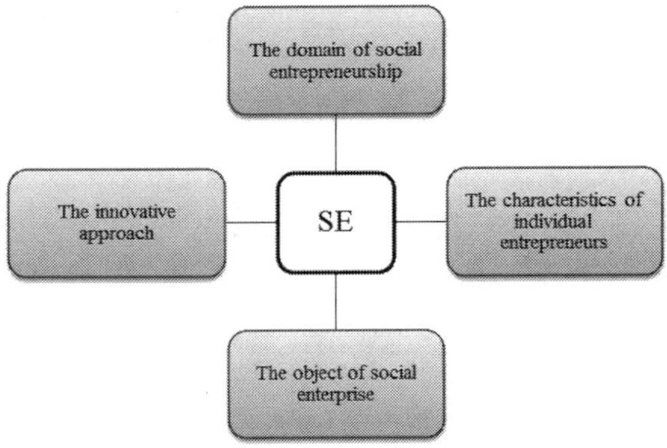

With such an unclear theoretical background is not surprising that sometimes even the terminology is an issue. For example, the terms “social entrepreneurship”, “social enterprise”, “social entrepreneur” and “social innovation” are sometimes used interchangeably, and are sometimes distinguished from one another. As this has been and will continue to be a source of confusion, it is important to underline the differences among the concepts. Definitions of social entrepreneurship typically refer to a process or behaviour, while definitions of social entrepreneurs focus instead on the founder of the initiative; and definitions of social enterprise refer to the tangible outcome of SE. These concepts are themselves different from the concept of social innovation that somehow includes them, as it refers to a process that aims to make a change at the systemic level (Westley and Antadze 2010).

As shown in Fig. 2.3, the analysis of the theoretical background of SE is here proposed using four variables according to which its definitions could be grouped: (1) the domain of social entrepreneurship, (2) the characteristics of individual social entrepreneurs, (3) the object of social enterprises, and (4) the innovative approach. In the following sections each of these aspects will be analysed and described according to their main issues and contributions.

2.3.1 The Domain of Social Entrepreneurship

The identification of a proper domain of SE is an important issue for scholars. Researchers do not agree on the field into which social enterprises fall, the for-profit or the non-profit sector, and this lead to conceptualizations of SE that are completely different from each other. The reasonableness of the debate lies in the fact that both approaches have advantages and disadvantages. As SE is still an evolving field of practice, it might be preferable not to narrowly define it, so as to avoid the risk of excluding initiatives that might need to be considered within the concept of SE, even if they do not meet all of the essential features. However, it is not completely correct to overly dilute the concept, as this may create confusion about how best to identify the phenomenon. The risk is indeed that the term could become very inclusive and thus represent an immense tent into which all kinds of socially beneficial activities fit.

Those who adopt a narrower approach define social enterprises as non-profit initiatives aimed at searching for alternative funding strategies based on the application of business expertise and market-based skills traditionally not related to the non-profit sector (Reis 1999; Thompson 2002). There is a large body of literature that locates the concept of SE within the world of non-profit organizations. For example, a survey of the appearance of the term "social entrepreneurship" in scholarly and non-scholarly publications over a 19-year period (1980–1999) suggested that 83 % of press references to SE cited examples from the non-profit sector. This appears to have been decisive in encouraging the authors of the survey to infer that SE is overwhelmingly a non-profit sector phenomenon (Taylor et al. 2000). Non-profit organizations may be interested in using managerial practices and behaviours because the environment within which they operate is rapidly changing due to increasing globalization, growing needs in their target communities, and a generally tighter funding environment with growing competition for donors and grants. This has led non-profit organizations to adopt a competitive position in their operations and to pursue innovative ways of delivering superior value to the target market and capturing competitive advantage. Furthermore, there is increasing interest from these organizations in searching for ways to avoid welfare dependency in program participants. As a consequence, non-profit organizations aspiring to achieve a competitive advantage must adopt an entrepreneurial view in their key decisions and build and nurture distinctive capabilities (Mort et al. 2003).

There is a branch of literature, however, for which SE is intended as innovative activities with a social objective that can also be developed by for-profits relying on commercial capital and concerned with financial returns (Mair and Marti 2006; Perrini 2007). From this perspective the central driver of SE is the social problem being addressed, and the legal form a social enterprise takes should be a decision based on the format that would most effectively mobilize the resources needed (Austin et al. 2006). In this wide view, SE is considered a new field of study rather than an advancement in the non-profit sector, the land of those innovators who contribute to social change with creativity and innovation (Perrini and Vurro 2006). The decision about which legal form to adopt depends on the single social entrepreneur and his perception of the one that could best suit his situation, but is a secondary concern (Dees and Anderson 2006). This inclusive definition of SE (Light 2009a) comprehends for-profit and non-profit organizations as well as some government initiatives, but it excludes those entities that exist only to provide social services and groups formed to engage in social activism (Swanson and Zhang 2010). Leadbeater (1997) conceptualized SE as the point of intersection between any two, or all three, sectors: public, private and voluntary.

Table 2.2 lists some examples of broad and narrow definitions.

Table 2.2 Examples of broad and narrow definitions

Perspective	Authors (Year)	Definition
Broad	OECD (1999)	Any private activity conducted in the public interest, organized with an entrepreneurial strategy but whose purpose is not the maximization of profit but attainment of certain economic and social goals
	Nicholls (2005)	SE may be defined as a professional, innovative, and sustainable approach to systemic change that resolves social market failures and grasps opportunities. Social entrepreneurs engage with a wide range of business and organizational models, both not-for- and for-profit, but the success of their activities is measured first and foremost by their social impact
	Haugh (2005)	Social enterprise is a collective term for a range of organizations that trade for a social purpose. They adopt one of a variety of different legal formats but have in common the principles of pursuing business-led solutions to achieve social aims, and the reinvestment of surplus for community benefit
	Mair and Martì (2006)	SE as innovative, social value creating activity that can occur within or across the non-profit, business or government sector
Narrow	Evans et al. (2001)	Social enterprises are not-for-profit organizations, which seek to meet social aims by engaging in economic and trading activities
	Mort et al. (2003)	As a special category of NGOs, social enterprises are not-for-profit organizations driven by a social mission
	Dart (2004)	SE differs from the traditional understanding of the non-profit organization in terms of strategy, structure, norms, values, and represents a radical innovation in the non-profit sector
	Simonov et al. (2014)	SE is innovative form of non-profit sector

2.3.2 Characteristics of Individual Entrepreneurs

A consistent branch of research is focused on the personality of social entrepreneurs. One of the reasons why many contributions focus on the features that best describe social entrepreneurs is that since SE is mission-related and internal values and motivation largely drive the venture (Hemingway 2005), it can be expected that the people involved will have specific skills and attitudes. Furthermore, defining SE is logically linked with defining social entrepreneurs in that entrepreneurship is what comes out from entrepreneurs' activities (Peredo and McLean 2006).

The main issue within this branch of research concerns the possibility of finding a common set of features that typically refer to social entrepreneurs. In doing so, scholars refer to the long tradition of studies on the personalities of entrepreneurs. Among its first delineations, the term "entrepreneur" appeared in economics as early as the 17th and 18th centuries, to define someone who undertakes a significant project or activity. Thus, being an entrepreneur involves much more than just starting a business. More specifically, the term came to be used to identify the venturesome individuals who stimulated economic progress by finding new and better ways of doing things (Dees 1998). The authors most commonly credited with giving it this particular meaning are Say and Schumpeter. Say (1803) described an entrepreneur as a person who shifts economic resources out of an area of lower productivity into an area of higher productivity and greater yield. On the same path, Schumpeter (1934) saw entrepreneurs as innovators who drive the creative-destructive process of capitalism—the change agents in the economy who move it forward to serve new markets, or who create new ways of doing things. Along the Say-Schumpeter lines of thinking, many contemporary authors have enriched the definition of the concept. An example is Drucker (1995), who took the notion of "opportunity" as central in defining the role of entrepreneurs: they have a mindset that sees the possibilities rather than the problems created by change. Stevenson and Jarillo (1990) added an element of resourcefulness to the definition. He suggested defining the heart of entrepreneurial management as the pursuit of opportunity without regard to the resources currently controlled. All these definitions encompass a much wider scope than the concept of business start-ups.

The definition of social entrepreneur is largely drawn from these studies. According to Zamagni (2006), social entrepreneurs are those individuals who have entrepreneurial virtues and follow market rules without aiming to achieve economic goals such as profit; rather, they strive to meet collective interests. Authors like Dees (1998), Drayton (2002) started from the aforementioned studies to prove the uniqueness of social entrepreneurs. They applied the entrepreneurial mindset to the pursuit of a social mission that leads to some distinctive challenges that ought to be reflected in the definitions. For this reason, their work is aimed at identifying the features that make social entrepreneurs a special breed of leaders (Dees 1998).

Many other authors have also focused their attention on defining the characteristics of social entrepreneurs, questioning for example whether they have special leadership skills (Thompson et al. 2000), greater passion to realize their vision (Bornstein 1998), or special charisma (Roper and Cheney 2005).

Table 2.3 shows a sample of definitions and traits that emerged in the literature review as belonging to social entrepreneurs.

Other authors find the definitions of Say, Schumpeter, Drucker, and Stevenson useful because they can be easily applied in the social as well as the business sector. Emphasizing how the entrepreneurial profile they describe can be manifested anywhere, they propose the assimilation of social entrepreneurs with traditional ones. Massetti (2008), for example, listed the main definitions of social entrepreneurs and pointed out how efforts to distinguish them from traditional entrepreneurs have led to findings of many more similarities than differences. As she stated, the evidence indicates that all entrepreneurs are passionate, driven individuals who believe that their ideas will make the world a better place, regardless of whether they receive the title of "social" entrepreneurs or not. An example she cites is that of Howard Schultz of Starbucks Coffee Company, who possesses many of the traits that social entrepreneurs are believed to have. He is a passionate, socially conscious individual who has based his coffee business on offering people a sense of community, comfort, and extended family. He is also the first entrepreneur in the US to

Table 2.3 Examples of definitions and traits of social entrepreneurs

Author (Year)	Definition of social entrepreneur	Traits
Drayton (2002)	Social entrepreneurs see something in society that is stuck, that is not working, and envision a systemic change that will allow them to shift society to a new and better way. They have a drive that will not stop until it is done	1. Possession of a powerful new system-changing idea
		2. Creativity
		3. Entrepreneurial spirit to drive change across society
		4. Strong ethical fibre
Mort et al. (2003)	Those who are driven by the social mission of creating better social value than their competitors which results in their displaying entrepreneurially virtuous behaviour	1. Balanced judgement
		2. A coherent unity of purpose and action in the face of stakeholder complexity
		3. Create better social value for clients
		4. Innovative
		5. Proactive
		6. Risk-taking propensity
		7. Passion
Roberts and Woods (2005)	SE is the construction, evaluation, and pursuit of opportunities for transformative social change carried out by visionary, passionately dedicated individuals	1. Passion
		2. Dogged persistence
		3. Creativity
		4. See things differently
		5. Recognize the importance of thinking like a business
Hartigan (2006)	Entrepreneurs whose work is aimed at progressive social transformation	1. Capacity to envisage what does not exist and make it happen
		2. Innovative
		3. Resourceful
		4. Opportunity aware
Light (2009b)	Social entrepreneurs are creating innovative ways of tackling some of our most pressing and intractable social problems […]. They take under-utilized and often discarded resources—people and building—and re-energize them by finding new ways to use them to satisfy unmet and often unrecognized needs	1. Entrepreneurial
		2. Innovative
		3. Transformatory
		4. Leader
		5. Storyteller
		6. People manager
		7. Visionary opportunist
		8. Alliance builder

provide stock options and healthcare access to part-time employees. Yet, he is commonly considered a well-intentioned, successful traditional entrepreneur, even if it is possible to affirm that he has all the traits traditionally recognized as belonging to social entrepreneurs.

From this perspective it does not appear that there is a distinguishing set of traits that delineate social from traditional entrepreneurs. What can be considered as the differentiating factor appears to be the nature of the mission that entrepreneurs select for their business: social entrepreneurs focus more on social concerns, while traditional entrepreneurs focus more on market-oriented ones. Nevertheless, both seek profit to drive their businesses forward and both seek to make important changes in the marketplace.

2.3.3 The Object of Social Enterprises

Defining the proper object of social enterprises is not easy because of their hybrid nature, in which elements from different fields are combined. The trend of identifying the boundaries of this phenomenon mainly consists of describing SE by underlining what it is not—those elements that differentiate this phenomenon from other well-known ones. However, even if a consensus on the boundaries of SE is difficult to find, the need to define them is strongly felt among scholars, so as to delimit their scope and clarify whether this really is an independent field of research (Swanson and Zhang 2010; Dacin et al. 2010).

The search for the object of these entities finds a certain accord among scholars, as opposed to the domain or the specificities of social entrepreneurs, on which different perspectives exist. Common across the definitions is the fact that the underlying drive of social enterprises is to create social value rather than personal and shareholder wealth. The disagreement is about the level of importance social entrepreneurs should place on the social mission. For example, the social mission may be the major focus of an organization, or profit may be the major motive of an organization that happens to provide some social product or service (Alter 2006). Some argue that having both social and economic value is important for social entrepreneurs (Emerson and Twersky 1996), while others suggest that economic value should be a limited concern for social entrepreneurs and the social mission must be central (Seelos and Mair 2007).

What emerges is that despite the different meanings this concept has in the definitions of SE, it is a feature that is always present in scholars' attempts to describe this phenomenon.

Table 2.4 lists some examples of definitions where the key role of social mission in defining SE emerges.

Table 2.4 Examples of definitions focusing on the key role of social mission

Author(s)	Year	Definition
Zadek and Thake	1997	The underlying drive for SE is to create social value, rather than personal and shareholder wealth […] The central driver for SE is the social problem being addressed, and the particular organizational form a social enterprise takes should be a decision based on which format would most effectively mobilize the resources needed
Alvord et al.	2004	SE creates innovative solutions to immediate social problems and mobilizes the ideas, capacities, resources and social arrangements required for sustainable social transformations
Hibbert et al.	2005	SE can be loosely defined as the use of entrepreneurial behaviours for social ends rather than for profit objectives, or alternatively, that the profits generated are used for the benefit of a specific disadvantaged group
Korosec and Berman	2006	SE is included in the process of individuals or of the private organizations that have the initiative to identify and solve social problems in order to develop new ways of solving social problems
Tracey and Jarvis	2007	The notion of trading for a social purpose is at the core of SE, requiring that social entrepreneurs identify and exploit market opportunities, and assemble the necessary resources, in order to develop products and/or services that allow them to generate "entrepreneurial profit" for a given social project

2.3.4 The Innovative Approach

The innovative approach that social entrepreneurs take when striving for social outcomes is a further element that is generally accepted by scholars as a common feature of social enterprises. Social entrepreneurs are described as those who involve "pattern-breaking" (Light 2006) or "innovative solutions" (Ashoka 2011) and are thus "change agents" (Schwab Foundation 2011) in society, rather than simple replicators of existing enterprises or practices (Austin et al. 2006).

Even in this case, the term "innovativeness" has different meanings. It could refer to products and services or processes, but also to innovative ways of delivering and promoting products and services, or to the innovative target addressed.

Table 2.5 lists some of the most important definitions in which the concept of innovation is highlighted.

The explicit role of innovation recalled in the definitions listed in Table X is consistent with the Schumpeterian view of entrepreneurship which, as aforementioned, emphasizes the role of innovation in entrepreneurship. However, as Schumpeter notes, innovation can take many forms. It does not require inventing something that is completely new; it can simply involve applying an existing idea in a new way or to a new situation. From this perspective entrepreneurs do not need to be inventors; they need to be creative in applying what others have already invented. Their innovations may appear in how they structure their core programs

Table 2.5 The role of innovation in defining SE

Author(s)	Year	Definition
Zadek and Thake	1997	The underlying drive for SE is […] that the activity is characterized by innovation, or the creation of something new rather than simply the replication of existing enterprises or practices
Austin et al.	2006	[SE] is innovative, social value creating activity that can occur within or across the non-profit, business, or government sectors
Light	2006	A social entrepreneur is an individual, group, network, organization, or alliance of organizations that seeks sustainable, large-scale change through pattern-breaking ideas in what or how governments, non-profit and business do to address significant social problems
Hartigan	2006	SE follows the transformation of entrepreneurship in a progressive way. This definition involves entirely new models, innovative, ingenious ones based on identifying opportunities
Tracey and Jarvis	2007	SE is the way of using resources to create benefits for the society and the SEur is the person who seeks to benefit society through innovation and risk-taking
OECD	2010	SE and social innovation […] aim to provide innovative solutions to unsolved social problems, putting social value creation at the heart of their mission in order to improve individuals' and communities' lives and increase their well-being

or in how they assemble their resources and fund their work. On the funding side, social entrepreneurs look for innovative ways to ensure that their ventures will have access to resources as long as they are creating social value. This willingness to innovate is part of the *modus operandi* of entrepreneurs as a continuous process of exploring, learning, and improving (Dees 1998).

Innovation is also considered a key element from a narrower perspective. When SE refers to the field of non-profit organizations, it still involves pursuing the path of innovation. In this case innovation is intended as a knowledge acquisition and integration process in which social enterprises learn from market changes, and involves monitoring changes in client preferences and competitor actions (Mort 2002). In their acquisition of profit-making skills and strategies, social enterprises within the non-profit sector indeed have an innovative approach.

2.4 Social Entrepreneurship Across Countries

The considerable debate on how to univocally define the phenomenon of SE has been considerably nurtured by the existing differences among definitions and concepts, as identified in regions around the world. The question of how the context in which it takes place can shape the development of a social enterprise and result in the identification of several elements in a country that can affect it. These elements mostly refer to specific socio-economic conditions (Kerlin 2009), existing institutions that can influence the growth of the non-profit sector (Salamon and Sokolowski 2010), and national trends in entrepreneurship that are connected with government and society (Bosma and Levie 2010). In particular, the state plays a key role in influencing the model of social enterprise. This is because the development of SE is influenced by the economic situation and civil society, which are in turn shaped by the state as a mix of culture, hierarchies, and political-economic histories(Kerlin 2013).

National influences may also have an impact on individual entrepreneurial decisions. Estrin et al. (2013) analysed the relation between social and commercial entrepreneurship, and theorized about national institutions that facilitate the emergence of both. They argue that the national prevalence rate of SE in a country positively influences the likelihood that individuals in that country will undertake commercial activity. Also, the quality of the institutional framework of a country equally influences social and commercial start-ups, while government activism has a negative influence, which is more marked for commercial than for social enterprises.

Analysing how SE is shaped within different contexts is important in that it allows us to identify macro-trends and make general statements about, for example, the likelihood of social enterprises taking place in a particular region, and the features of these enterprises. Mostly, literature on social enterprise in relation to places focuses on single-country or regional analysis, and/or case studies, rather than a global comparison (Bagnoli and Megali 2011; Grieco 2014). Important exceptions come from the work of the Global Entrepreneurship Monitor (GEM). The GEM research is carried out every year with the explicit objective to facilitate cross-country comparisons of entrepreneurial activity by surveying representative population samples of at least 2000 randomly selected adults in the participating countries. In 2009, additional questions were included to assess the entity of social entrepreneurial activities within the analysed sample. With more than 150,000 individuals in 49 countries, this report produces unique insights, as it represents the first global and harmonized assessment of this phenomenon. The whole sample was asked about the current or potential involvement in any kind of activity, organization or initiative that has a particularly social, environmental or community objective. Those who answered positively numbered 8774 (less than 5 % of the whole sample), almost equally divided into actual owners and potential start-ups of social enterprises. Afterwards, a series of follow-up questions was administered to both groups in order to gauge the extent of innovation, reliance on market-based revenues and importance attached to societal objectives.

This research provides data on how social enterprises are established at a worldwide level. What emerges is that social entrepreneurs are still a rare breed. The average rate of SE activities across all 49 countries in the sample is 1.9 % (ranging from 0.2 to 4.9 %). It has to be considered, however, that these results refer to 2009, while more recent years have seen a great development of SE, both in terms of literature on the topic and structured organizations. Concerning the relation between social enterprises and places, the authors suggest grouping countries by stage of development, adopting an unusual distinction between factor-driven countries, efficiency-based countries and innovation-driven countries. The first group refers to those economies that are based on the exploitation of natural resources, the second comprises those economies mostly based on large-scale manufacturing, while third group includes those economies that are based on services and innovation. According to this classification, even if the average number of SE activities is similar for the three groups of countries, the rate seems to increase slightly with economic development (factor-driven: 1.5; efficiency-based: 2.0; innovation-based: 2.1). This may indicate that the opportunity-cost of SE is higher in developing countries, because other goals related to fundamental self-interests need to be satisfied first (Lepoutre et al. 2013).

This study reveals that in most countries the majority of social enterprises are at an early stage of development (under 42 months), with the exception of Italy and Germany, where the rate of early-stage and established social enterprises is the same (OECD 2013), (see Fig. 2.4).

Again, it has to be considered that this data refers to 2009, and that important growth is still happening; thus it is reasonable to presume that the highlighted trends would be different if the same study were replicated today. Nevertheless, the GEM survey is worth citing as it is among the widest studies on SE, and able to capture general trends that emerge at a worldwide level.

Several studies have focused on SE in Europe and the differences between the configuration of the phenomenon both there and in the US. Social enterprises in Europe had their first appearance with the Italian law on cooperatives in 1991. In the latter part of the decade the concept was introduced in several other European countries to reflect the entrepreneurial approaches adopted by non-profit organizations. However, differences can be seen in the ways the same term was used to refer to different types of organizations: in countries like France, Portugal, Spain and Greece there was a strong predominance of the cooperative model, while in

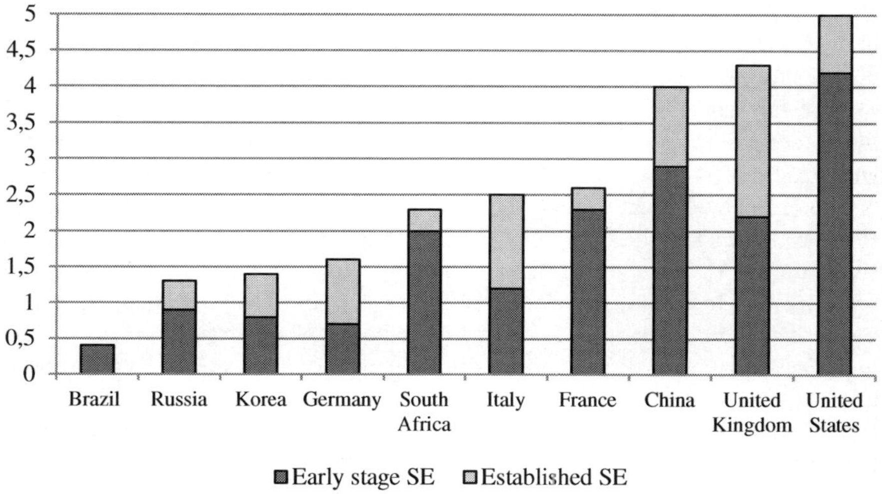

Fig. 2.4 Social entrepreneurship prevalence rate as a percentage of the working age population by enterprise maturity. Adapted by Lepoutre et al. (2013)

countries like Belgium, the UK and Italy (with the law of 2006) the focus was no longer on cooperatives, but on more open models of enterprise that were adopted (Defourny and Nyssens 2013). A specific trend during the 1990s was to consider social enterprises as organizations with the purpose of including disadvantaged categories in the workforce. This type of social enterprise was indeed quite dominant across Europe, most of all in the Bismarckian countries that were the first to develop this scheme, and in countries like Finland and Poland where the laws on SE specifically refer to programs targeting the field of work integration.

The distribution of social enterprises across Europe, and the weight and focus they have, are highly variable from country to country. In Italy, for example, there is a large number of social enterprises working in several different fields. In counties like Sweden and Finland their number is considerable, but they are active in specific fields such as employment and kindergartens. Germany and Denmark, on the other hand, have a small number of social enterprises and, along with the Netherlands, are examples of countries where existing social enterprises are not clearly differentiated from public or third-sector organizations (Borzaga and Defourny 2001).

In the US, where the welfare state was comparatively weak, the emergence of social enterprises was shaped by a bottom-up approach, and a process of development was primarily fronted by a voluntary sector. In its first manifestation the debate on SE started with the use of commercial activities by non-profit organizations, a behaviour that can be traced back to the very foundation of the US, when community or religious groups sold goods to supplement voluntary donations. This behaviour gained particular importance between the 1970s and 1980s, when significant funds were addressed to education, healthcare, community development and poverty programs through the activities of non-profit organizations working in these areas, instead of public institutions. This support started to fail in the late 1970s with the downturn in the economy, prompting non-profit organizations to fill the gap in the budget through the sale of goods and services, even when this was not directly related to their mission.

A feature common to both Europe and the US is that the development of SE started around entrepreneurial behaviours with a social mission, arising primarily within the non-profit sector. Important differences, however, are traceable both in the origins and in the key actors involved. In Europe the third sector has always played a significant role in providing welfare services, and this trend took a prominent role in supporting new forms of hiring or retraining unemployed people in non-profit organizations. In the US, social enterprises emerged from a combination of decrease in public support and increase in commercial income. Also, the actors involved show important differences: while cooperatives and new forms of work integration played a key role in the development of European social enterprises, in the US the main contributions came from foundations that provided financial support and visibility for social entrepreneurs, and consultancy firms that developed a growing industry focusing on adapting business methods and strategies to the needs of these innovative non-profits (Kerlin 2006; Defourny and Nyssens 2013).

2.5 The Path for Future Development

The call for further research has been widely expressed in the hope of moving the field of SE study towards the next steps of development. In line with the general requests to continue investigating this topic in order to definitely establish it as an autonomous branch of research (Mair and Marti 2006; Peredo and McLean 2006; Nicholls 2006), two main paths are identifiable, both of them focused on the need to find a way to measure the phenomenon of SE.

In one sense, measuring SE means mapping social enterprises in their emergence and development across different contexts. From this perspective the need is twofold. First, common criteria have to be identified to univocally define the concept and overcome the mismatching arising from the different meanings given to SE. As long as a general understanding of this phenomenon is lacking, severe barriers would hinder the possibility of implementing quantitative studies on social enterprises. This is indeed the second element that must be improved: in addressing the topic of SE, conceptual articles greatly outnumber empirical studies, and empirical efforts often lack formal hypotheses and rigorous methodology (Short et al. 2009). The majority of existing contributions focus on defining the concept, and this has of course been very useful in the initial stages. However, the current need is to evolve the approach and put effort into empirically investigating the phenomenon. Case study analyses comprise the majority of existing attempts at empirical study. These works have played a pivotal role in accurately and specifically giving insights into the actual behaviours of social enterprises, but they lack the ability to offer generalizable findings, keeping SE research in a developmental state.

Measuring SE also means finding a way to assess the performance of social enterprises. There is much debate on this issue, as instruments to assess the performance of for-profit organizations are not able to capture the whole picture of social enterprises, which leverage economic activities for the pursuit of a social mission and thus cannot be evaluated regardless of their ability to create social value. Social enterprises have huge potential to generate impact at the societal, environmental and economic levels, and it is essential for them to monitor and evaluate this impact. Also, as their driving mission is to solve social problems, they must be sure about the actual achievement of this mission. This is the reason why impact assessment takes on a pivotal meaning for these organizations.

The measurement of performance and consequent impact at economic, environmental and social levels are among the most important challenges for studies in the field of SE. The main issue is not the measurement itself, but the conversion of mostly qualitative data related to the achievement of a social mission into quantitative metrics. The need for identifying suitable indicators to measure social outcomes is widely felt not only in the third sector but in other sectors as well. In for-profit companies, for example, the increase in this trend is directly linked with the growing importance given to CSR activities and the consequent need for proper measuring indices. Since the concept of sustainable development was coined by the Brundtland Commission's report (1987), sustainability has been adopted by many companies through their mission statement and strategy, which raises the issue of how to incorporate the social and environmental dimensions of sustainability in programs and projects. The same requirement is also emerging in the public sector, where efforts are limited to the health sector and, to a lesser extent, to the care sector (Zappalà and Lyons 2009).

This topic is not new for social enterprises or, more widely, for the third sector. Compared with the past, the difference stems from the new competitive context faced by these organizations, which requires proper assessment of the generated impact to improve performance and communicate the benefits in an effective manner. Assigning the right importance to social items is of relevance for non-profit organizations because some of these organizations serve their clients either without charge or with a nominal charge, and therefore the financial statements do not track the benefits created. Moreover, even non-profit organizations with earned revenues have a social mission, and therefore including social benefits in the financial statements is necessary to provide a more complete view of the overall performance (Richmond et al. 2003). Thus, focusing on financial management can be meaningless for social enterprises, as it is not a concern of their purposes and missions. The cost-revenue strategies for profit maximization do not fit with the social enterprise model, which has several bottom lines.

The concept of social impact assessment (SIA) is thus emerging, with particular urgency for social enterprises. Among the main paths for future development, the consolidation of this practice within this specific field, and the question of which definition of processes and indicators to adopt, are of great relevance. However, the attempt to move towards a different perspective from that of traditional economics collides with a deep-rooted belief about the high complexity of measuring and quantifying the creation of social value (Arvidson et al. 2010; Porter et al. 2012). Even if generally accepted accounting principles exist to aid financial reporting, a comparable standard related to the measurement and communication of social impact does not yet exist because it is difficult to universally define the concept, and the related measurement tools often lack the rigour that characterizes scientific approaches aimed at assessing financial returns. Furthermore, the limited resources, the complexity of operationalizing impact, and organizational challenges in collecting and analysing data over time are among the main issues that hamper the implementation of these practices, especially among small and medium social enterprises (Barraket and Yousefpour 2013).

Nevertheless, despite the undeniable difficulties, an efficient assessment method offers many strategic opportunities for social entrepreneurs. Firstly, it provides a process that can improve the organization's performance because it enables a deep understanding of how best to allocate resources to maximize social outcomes. Understanding how activities create value and whom they benefit can help organizations design better targeted programs, and increase their effectiveness by improving what works and eliminating what does not (KPMG 2014). Furthermore, it enables improved accounting practices and enhanced organizational legitimacy within its stakeholder network (Dart 2004). SIA plays an important role in enhancing stakeholder involvement because it foresees listening to feedback from the beneficiaries of the implemented activities as well as the other directly or indirectly involved parties. Furthermore, as SIA provides information related to the way in which the received investments are used in addressing social issues, this communication is highly strategic, especially in a context of increasingly competitive fundraising. To this end, the interest of those who fund these organizations in supporting the promoted social cause is highly important, and the existence of shared practices aimed at better assessing and communicating social outcomes is relevant for the evaluation of projects in which to invest (Porter et al. 2012; Ruttman 2012). This is a key aspect because the investment sector plays a unique role in promoting ethical practices throughout the economy.

Given this importance, efforts have been and should be made to enhance the development of the practice. Understanding how to strengthen SIA processes can be a promising avenue for future research on social enterprises, to help entrepreneurs understand the best ways to allocate their resources for the achievement of the social mission and to enable social enterprises to benefit from innovative sources of funding, where reporting the generated outcomes is the main criterion for the awarding of grants.

References

Alter, K. (2006). A social enterprise typology. *Virtue Ventures*. http://virtueventures.com. Accessed 15 May 2013.

Alvord, S. H., Brown, L. D., & Letts, C. W. (2004). Social entrepreneurship and societal transformation an exploratory study. *The Journal of Applied Behavioral Science, 40*(3), 260–282.

Arvidson, M., Lyon, F., McKay, S., & Moro, D. (2010). The ambitions and challenges of SROI.

Ashoka. (2011). http://www.ashoka.org/. Accessed 28 Apr 2013.

Austin, J., Gutierrez, R., Ogliastri, E., & Reficco, E. (2006). *Effective management of social enterprises: Lessons from businesses and civil society organizations in Iberoamerica*. Cambridge: Harvard University.

Bagnoli, L., & Megali, C. (2011). Measuring performance in social enterprises. *Non-profit and Voluntary Sector Quarterly, 40*(1), 149–165.

Barraket, J., & Yousefpour, N. (2013). Evaluation and social impact measurement amongst small to medium social enterprises: Process, purpose and value. *Australian Journal of Public Administration, 72*(4), 447–458.

Bornstein, D. (1998). Changing the world on a shoestring. *Atlantic Monthly, 281*(1), 34–39.

Bornstein, D. (2004). *How to change the world: Social entrepreneurs and the power of new ideas*. Oxford: Oxford University Press.

Borzaga, C., & Defourny, J. (Eds.). (2001). *The emergence of social enterprise*. USA: Routledge.

Borzaga, C., Bodini, R., Carini, C., Depedri, S., Galera, G., & Salvatori, G. (2014). *Europe in transition: The role of social cooperatives and social enterprises*, Euricse Working Papers, 69| 14.

Bosma, N., & Levie, J. (2010). *Global Entrepreneurship Monitor 2009 Global Report*. http://static.wamda.com/web/uploads/resources/GEM_2009_Global_Report_Rev_140410.pdf

Carini, C., & Costa, E. (2013). *Exploring the performance of social cooperatives during the economic crisis: The Italian case*. Italy: Euricse Working Paper.

Castellano, F. L. (2003). Una sociedad "de cambio y no de beneficencia". El asociacio-nismo en la España liberal. *CIRIEC-ESPAÑA, 44*, 199–228.
Certo, S. T., & Miller, T. (2008). Social entrepreneurship: Key issues and concepts. *Business Horizons, 51*, 267–271.
Chaves, R., & Monzón, J. L. (2012). The social economy in the European Union. *European Economic and Social Committee*, 1–116.
Dacin, P., Dacin, M., & Matear, M. (2010). Social entrepreneurship: Why we don't need a new theory and how we move forward from here. *The Academy of Management Perspectives, 3*, 37–57.
Dart, R. (2004). The legitimacy of social enterprise. *Non-profit Management and Leadership, 14* (4), 411–424.
Dees, J. G. (1998). *The meaning of social entrepreneurship*. Comments and suggestions contributed from the Social Entrepreneurship Funders Working Group, 6 p.
Dees, J. G., & Anderson, B. B. (2006). Framing a theory of social entrepreneurship: Building on two schools of practice and thought. *Research on Social Entrepreneurship: Understanding and Contributing to an Emerging Field, 1*(3), 39–66.
Defourny, J., & Nyssens, M. (2013). Social co-operatives: When social enterprises meet the co-operative tradition. *Journal of Entrepreneurial and Organizational Diversity, 2*(2), 11–33.
Drayton, W. (2002). The citizen sector: Becoming as entrepreneurial and competitive as business. *California Management Review, 44*(3), 120–132.
Drucker, P. (1995). *Innovation and entrepreneurship*. New York: Harper Business, *28*.
Eckhardt, J. T., & Shane, S. A. (2003). Opportunities and entrepreneurship. *Journal of Management, 29*(3), 333–349.
Emerson, J., & Twersky, F. (1996). *New social entrepreneurs: The success, challenge and lessons of non-profit enterprise creation*. San Francisco.
Estrin, S., Mickiewicz, T., & Stephan, U. (2013). Entrepreneurship, social capital, and institutions: Social and commercial entrepreneurship across nations. *Entrepreneurship Theory and Practice, 37*(3), 479–504.
Euricse. (2013). Social economy and social entrepreneurship, Social Europe Guide, *4*.
Eurostat. (2013). *People at risk of poverty or social exclusion*. http://epp.eurostat.ec.europa.eu
Fondazione, L. (2007). *Nuove povertà ed esclusione sociale*. http://zope.unimc.it/netmate/seminari/primo/nuovepovert.pdf
Grieco, C. (2014). Exploring Italian social enterprises coherence in social impact assessment Conference Proceedings Euram Annual Conference, Valencia, 4–7 June 2014.
Hartigan, P. (2006). It's about people, not profits. *Business Strategy Review, 17*(4), 42–45.
Haugh, H. (2005). A research agenda for social entrepreneurship. *Social Enterprise Journal, 1*(1), 1–12.
Hemingway, C. A. (2005). Personal values as a catalyst for corporate social entrepreneurship. *Journal of Business Ethics, 60*(3), 233–249.
Hibbert, S. A., Hogg, G., & Quinn, T. (2005). Social entrepreneurship: Understanding consumer motives for buying the big issue. *Journal of Consumer Behaviour, 4*(3), 159–172.
Kerlin, J. A. (2006). Social enterprise in the United States and Europe: Understanding and learning from the differences. *Voluntas, 17*, 247–263.
Kerlin, J. A. (2013). Defining social enterprise across different contexts: A conceptual framework based on institutional factors. *Nonprofit and Voluntary Sector Quarterly, 42*(1), 84–108.
Kerlin, J. A. (Ed.). (2009). *Social enterprise: A global comparison*. Lebanon: Tufts University Press.
Korosec, R. L., & Berman, E. M. (2006). Municipal support for social entrepreneurship. *Public Administration Review, 66*, 448–462.
KPMG International. (2014). *Sustainable insight*. Unlocking the value of social investment. kpmg.com/sustainability.
Kraus, S., Filser, M., O'Dwyer, M., & Shaw, E. (2013). Social entrepreneurship: An exploratory citation analysis. *Review of Managerial Science*, 1–18.
Leadbeater, C. (1997). The rise of the social entrepreneur (No. 25). Demos.

Lepoutre, J., Justo, R., Terjesen, S., & Bosma, N. (2013). Designing a global standardized methodology for measuring social entrepreneurship activity: The global entrepreneurship monitor social entrepreneurship study. *Small Business Economics, 40*(3), 693–714.

Light, P. C. (2006). Reshaping social entrepreneurship. *Stanford Social Innovation Review, Fall*, 46–51.

Light, P. C. (2009a). *The search for social entrepreneurship*. Washington, D.C.: Brookings Institution Press.

Light, P. C. (2009b). Social entrepreneurship revisited: Not just anyone, anywhere, in any organization can make breakthrough change. *Stanford Social Innovation Review*, Summer, 21–22.

Mair J., & Marti J. (2006). Social entrepreneurships research: A source of explanation, prediction and delight. International Journal of World Business, *1*, 36–44.

Mair, J., Battilana, J., & Cardenas, J. (2012). Organizing for society: A typology of social entrepreneuring models. *Journal of Business Ethics, 111*(3), 353–373.

Massetti, B. L. (2008). The social entrepreneurship matrix as a "tipping point" for economic change. E:CO, *3*, 1–8.

Mort, G., Weerawardena, J., & Carnegie, K. (2003). Social entrepreneurship: Towards conceptualization. *International Journal of Non-profit and Voluntary Sector Marketing, 8*(1), 76–88.

Murphy, P. J., & Coombes, S. M. (2009). A model of social entrepreneurial discovery. *Journal of Business Ethics, 87*, 325–336.

Nicholls, A. (2005). *Measuring impact in social entrepreneurship New accountabilities to stakeholders and investors? skoll centre for social entrepreneurship*. Oxford: University of Oxford.

Nicholls, A. (Ed.). (2006). *Social entrepreneurship: New models of sustainable social change: New models of sustainable social change*. OUP: Oxford.

OECD. (2013). OECD Economic surveys Italy.

OECD. (2010). SMEs, Entrepreneurship and Innovation.

OECD. (1999). *Social enterprises*. Paris: OECD.

Peredo, A. M., & Mclean, M. (2006). Social entrepreneurship: A critical review of the concept. *Journal of World Business, 41*(1), 56–65.

Perrini, F. (2007). *Social entrepreneurship*. Milano: Egea.

Perrini, F., & Vurro, C. (2006) Social entrepreneurship: Innovation and social change across theory and practice. In: J. Mair, J. Robinson, K. Hockerts (Eds.), *Social Entrepreneurship* (pp. 57–85), UK: Palgrave Macmillan.

Pless, N. M. (2012). Social entrepreneurship in theory and practice—an introduction. *Journal of Business Ethics*, 1–4.

Porter M. E., & Kramer M. R. (2006). Strategy and Society. The link between competitive advantage and corporate social responsibility. *Harvard Business Review*, 78–92.

Porter, M. E, & Kramer M. R. (2011). Creating shared value. *Harvard Business Review*, 62–77

Porter, M. E., Hills, G., Pfitzer, M., Patscheke, S., & Hawkins, E. (2012). Measuring shared value how to unlock value by linking social and business results, *FSG*. http://www.fsg.org/Portals/0/Uploads/Documents/PDF/Measuring_Shared_Value.pdf

Reis, T. (1999). *Unleashing the new resources and entrepreneurship for the common good: A scan, synthesis and scenario for action* (p. 27). Battle Creek: W.K. Kellogg Foundation.

Restakis, J. (2006). Defining the social economy-the BC context. Prepared for: BC Social Economy Roundtable.

Richmond, B. J, Mook, L., & Quarter, J. (2003). Social accounting for non profits: Two models. *Non-profit Management and Leadership, 13*(4).

Roberts, D., & Woods, C. (2005). Changing the world on a shoestring: The concept of social entrepreneurship. *University of Auckland Business Review*, *7*(1), 45–51.

Roper, J., & Cheney, G. (2005). The meanings of social entrepreneurship today. *Corporate Governance, 5*(3), 95–104.

Ruttman, R. (2012). New ways to invest for social and environmental impact In *Investing for impact: How social entrepreneurship is redefining the meaning of return.* Credit Suisse Research.

Salamon, L., & Sokolowski, S. (2010). *The social origins of civil society: Explaining variations in the size and structure of the global civil society sector.* Paper presented at the 9th International Conference of the International Society for Third Sector Research, Istanbul, Turkey.

Santos, F. M. (2012). A positive theory of social entrepreneurship. *Journal of Business Ethics, 111* (3), 335–351.

Say, J. B. (1803). Traité d'économie politique: ou, simple exposition de la manière dont se forment, se distribuent et se consomment les richesses. (Translation: Treatise on Political Economy: On the Production, Distribution and Consumption of Wealth). New York: Kelley (1964) (1st ed., 1827).

Schumpeter, J. (1934). *The theory of economic development.* Cambridge: Harvard University Press.

Schwab Foundation. (2011). Social entrepreneur of the year India 2011, Social Entrepreneurship for Inclusive Growth. http://www.jubilantbhartiafoundation.com/seoy-profile-booklet-2011.pdf

Seelos, C., & Mair, J. (2007). Profitable business models and market creation in the context of deep poverty: A strategic view. *The Academy of Management Perspectives, 21*(4), 49–63.

Shaw, E., Gordon, J., Harvey, C., & Maclean, M. (2013). Exploring contemporary entrepreneurial philanthropy. *International Small Business Journal, 31*(5), 580–599.

Short, J. C., Moss, T. W., & Lumpkin, G. T. (2009). Research in social entrepreneurship: Past contributions and future opportunities. *Strategic Entrepreneurship Journal, 3*(2), 161–194.

Simonov, S. G., Khamatkhanova, M. A., & Peshkova, N. N. (2014). Development of social entrepreneurship on a given territory. *Life Science Journal, 11*(7 s).

Stevenson, H. H., & Jarillo, C. (1990). A paradigm of entrepreneurship: Entrepreneurial management. *Strategic Management Journal, 11*(Summer), 17–27.

Swanson, L. A., & Zhang, D. D. (2010). The social entrepreneurship zone. *Journal of Non-profit and Public Sector Marketing, 22*(2), 71–88.

Taylor, N., Hobbs, R., Nilsson, F., O'Halloran, K., & Preisser, C. (2000). The rise of the term social entrepreneurship in print publications. *In Frontiers of Entrepreneurship Research: proceedings of the annual Babson College Entrepreneurship Research Conference* (Vol. 466).

Thomas, A. (2004). The rise of social cooperatives in Italy. *Voluntas: International Journal of Voluntary and Non-profit Organizations, 15*(3), 243–263.

Thompson, J. (2002). The world of the social entrepreneur. *International Journal of Public Sector Management, 15*(5), 412–431.

Thompson, J., Alvy, G., & Less, A. (2000). Social entrepreneurship: A new look at the people and the potential. *Management Decision, 38*(5), 328–338.

Tracey, P., & Jarvis, O. (2007). Toward a theory of social venture franchising. *Entrepreneurship Theory and Practice, 31*(5), 667–685.

Weerawardena, J., & Mort, G. S. (2006). Investigating social entrepreneurship: A multidimensional model. *Journal of World Business, 41*(1), 21–35.

Westley, F., & Antadze, N. (2010). *Making a difference: Strategies for scaling social innovation for greater impact.* London: Routledge.

Yunus, M. (2003). *Banker to the poor: The story of the Grameen Bank.* Aurum Press Limited.

Zadek, S., & Thake, S. (1997). Send in the social entrepreneurs. *New Statesman, 26*(7339), 9–31.

Zamagni, S. (2006). Dalla filantropia d'impresa all'imprenditorialità sociale. East, 6.

Zappalà, G., & Lyons, M. (2009). Recent approaches to measuring social impact in the third sector: An overview. Centre for Social Impact, Background Paper, n. 5. http://www.socialauditnetwork.org.uk/files/8913/2938/6375/CSI_Background_Paper_No_5_-_Approaches_to_measuring_social_impact_-_150210.pdf

Chapter 3
Is Doing Good, Good Enough?

Assessing Social Impact

Abstract In this chapter the topic of social impact assessment (SIA) is addressed in its meanings and implications. It firstly explains how it has become important for both profit and non-profit organizations. Also, along with a detailed definition of what social impact actually means and an examination of the role the measurement process can have, the benefits that could come from this practice are illustrated, as well as the main barriers that could hamper its implementation. A specific focus is on the impact investment that has emerged in several countries witnessing the trend of using investment models to solve social needs. The pivotal role of SIA in relation to these tools is also explained in this chapter.

Keywords Social impact · Assessment process · Social accounting · Impact investing · Social impact bonds

3.1 From Financial Reporting to Social Accounting

The world of non-profit organizations, philanthropy and social enterprises has gone through two main trends of reporting activities in recent years. The first is the growing increase of accountability practices, with funders, taxpayers, concerned citizens and clients asking organizations to be more transparent about their fund-raising and spending, their governance assets, and the results achieved with the resources entrusted to them (Ebraim and Weisband 2007). The term "accountability" refers to an actor, whether an individual or an organization, who recognizes that it has made a promise to do something, and has accepted a moral and legal responsibility to do its best to fulfil that promise (Cutt and Murray 2002). An actor could feel and act as though it were accountable to an abstract purpose. It is quite common for non-profit organizations to be accountable for the achievement of intangible goals such as the advancement of human rights or the increase of social cohesion for disadvantaged categories. From this perspective their primary accountability is to the cause, and the expectations of other categories of stakeholders are fulfilled to the

C. Grieco, *Assessing Social Impact of Social Enterprises*,
SpringerBriefs in Business, DOI 10.1007/978-3-319-15314-8_3

extent that they align with the achievement of this mission. More generally, however, as accountability involves a promise to perform, it refers to a concrete relationship between two or more parties in which one party is accountable to another for the execution of some promised duty. The moral value of accountability may also include a requirement that an actor make it easy for the stakeholders to monitor the extent to which it has lived up to its promises, through a more or less continued reporting activity (Brown and Moore 2001).

The second and more recent trend concerned a shifting of the focus of reporting activities from accountability to the more specific concept of impact, requiring organizations to demonstrate results in addressing complex social issues such as poverty and inequality. This renewed attention to impact is driven both by funders who want to know whether their funds are making a difference or might be better spent elsewhere, as well as by committed non-profit leaders and social entrepreneurs looking for solutions to pressing societal problems (Ebrahim and Rangan 2010). Today, organizations are interested not only in assessing their economic output but also in measuring their impact on the surrounding area and communities. The call for a more complete view on organizations' activities is directed to for-profit as well as non-profit organizations, and both public and private entities. Stakeholder interest in the reporting of such information is substantial, but it involves severe difficulties. This is particularly true for those organizations with a social mission that have to find a way to translate qualitative outcomes, such as a reduction of social exclusion or increased self-esteem, into quantifiable and measurable data. Sawhill and Williamson (2001) discovered that the more abstract a not-for-profit mission was, the more difficult it was for them to develop usable measures of impacts.

The concept of social impact assessment has its roots in these trends and needs, and is currently becoming even more relevant, given the spread of phenomena such as impact investing. Originally, SIA was considered as a technique for predicting social impact as a component of the wider process of the environmental impact assessment (EIA). Although the EIA was intended as an all-inclusive framework for the consideration of non-economic results, both environmental and social, it failed to adequately address the social issues; thus SIA was developed with a gradual extension of the items under consideration. The role of SIA within the broader context of EIA has long been marginal, as shown by several studies that indicate it as the "lesser sibling" (Hildebrandt and Sandham 2014). However, its focus on the social well-being of societies has become an area of increasing concern in recent decades, leading SIA to an accelerated development.

The increase in SIA practices goes back to the 1970s. By this time, development agencies had begun to use impact assessment to approve, adjust or reject projects according to their likely environmental, social and economic consequences. In this first wave, non-financial reporting received considerable academic and managerial interest. In Europe, social reporting occurred most frequently in Germany, the Netherlands, and France. European reports focused mostly on employee matters and less on local community and environmental impacts, and contained mostly quantitative information (Kolk 2005). Overall, however, this phenomenon did not last long: in the 1980s social reporting lost momentum because it was not institutionalized (Diekers and Antal 1986). Attention shifted more to the economy, market-oriented policies emerged, and accountability on social and environmental issues apparently became less important. However, the first movement for accountability did lead to the emergence of several reporting models and standards (Epstein et al. 1976). In the late 1980s a second wave of reporting on non-financial issues emerged, with a particular focus on environmental issues and with most attention being paid to external accountability dimensions, which were greatly influenced by pressure from non-governmental organizations. Since then this practice has grown substantially, particularly in the form of separate reports (economic, environmental and social). By the 1990s social science professionals were also able to develop an acceptable set of SIA guidelines and principles that contributed to making it a component of the formal planning processes in most developed organizations over time (Richmond et al. 2003).

3.2 Developed Theories and Induced Behaviours of Social Awareness

Several studies on SIA have focused on the growing attention that organizations within both the for-profit and non-profit sectors should give it in relation to social wellness and development. In particular, four main approaches to the study of SIA have been presented: the Stakeholder Theory, the principle of Shared Value Creation, the concept of Triple Bottom Line, and the Blended Value Proposition. It is evident that even if these studies have different starting points (e.g. CSR strategy development, investment sector), they all developed on the basis of a dichotomous perspective of elements that they want to merge. Their goal is to understand how the economic and social elements should be integrated and fully assessed to maximize both social and financial value creation as well as shareholder returns. This takes on a role that is even more important when applied to social enterprises, which are both market-oriented and social mission-centred. Social enterprises thus combine economic and social values and manage the tensions arising from their co-existence (Le Ber et al. 2010).

Figure 3.1 shows how the aforementioned approaches can be intended as parts of a wider process of SIA that involves organizations increasing awareness of the effects they are having on society, both positive and negative. In doing so, stakeholder engagement becomes essential for understanding needs and expectations as well as the way in which these are impacted by organizations' activities. From this perspective the relation with stakeholders is a deep dialogue aimed at working together to solve the addressed social issue and create shared value. Thus the overall assessment cannot be focused only on the economic results; rather, it must include both societal and environmental outcomes.

In the following sections each approach will be described in more detail, focusing on its connection with the concept of SIA.

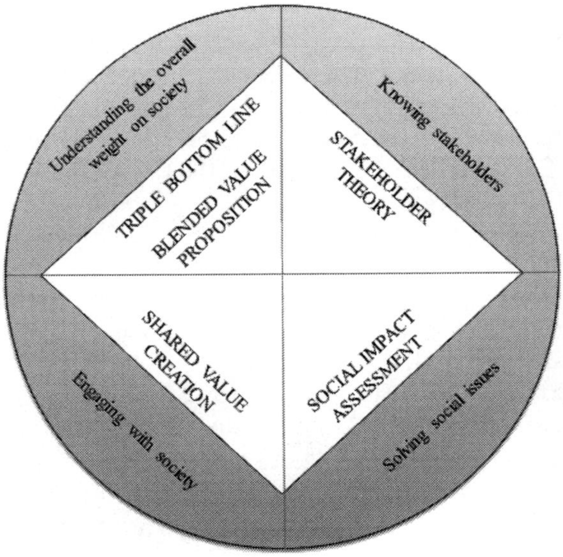

Fig. 3.1 Developed theories and induced behaviours of social awareness

3.2.1 Stakeholder Theory

In 1980s the firm was seen as belonging to the shareholders; its performance was therefore measured using shareholder return as the main evaluation indicator (Porter 1980). Then in the early 1990s a different view began to prevail: firms started to be seen as having responsibilities to a wider range of actors, rather than simply to shareholders, and a stakeholder-based perspective became gradually dominant (Post et al. 2002; Brown and Fraser 2006). Stakeholders may be defined as any individual, group or organization that is affected by or can affect the achievement of corporate actions, decisions, policies or goals. This includes groups such as shareholders, creditors, suppliers, the government, customers, competitors, employees, employees' families, the media, the local community, local charities, and also future generations. Corporate sustainability—the firm's ability to continue operating over a long period of time—depends upon the sustainability of its stakeholder relationships (Perrini et al. 2007). According to Gray et al. (1996), stakeholders are identified by companies and by reference to the extent of corporate beliefs; the interplay with each group therefore needs to be managed in order to further the interests of the corporation. Stakeholder theory recognizes that organizations have obligations not only to shareholders but also to these other interest groups.

Burton and Dunn (1996) explain that stakeholder theory refers to the management of the relationship between quality, care, and need. Stakeholder theory suggests that companies will manage such relationships based on different factors such as the nature of the task environment, the salience of stakeholder groups, and the values of decision-makers who determine the shareholder ranking process. Stakeholder theory has two branches: ethical and managerial (Deegan 2002). The ethical branch concerns the rights of all the stakeholders to assess information, and these rights should not be violated, as their acknowledgement can lead to improved corporate financial performance. The second branch refers to the commitment of corporate management to satisfying the information demands of those stakeholders who are important to its ongoing survival. It all depends on the idea that stakeholder expectations will impact on corporate operations and disclosure policies, so corporations are called upon to respond to these concerns.

Stakeholder theory naturally requires a systematic stakeholder analysis approach, whereby the organizations interact with stakeholders to identify their key expectations and areas of concern. This is important for non-profit organizations, and even more for social enterprises, as their hybrid nature means they have many different stakeholders to whom they must account (Bagnoli and Megali 2011). These organizations may indeed by accountable to donors for the proper handling of donated resources; to clients and beneficiaries for the delivery of high-quality, responsive services; to staff for continued support of the mission that drew them to the organization; and to partners and allies, for living up to commitments for action made in the course of developing and executing a joint project (Brown and Moore 2001).

3.2.2 Shared Value Creation

Moving from the field of CSR, Porter and Kramer (2006, 2011) noted that the prevailing approaches are fragmented and disconnected from business and strategy, thus causing some of the best opportunities for companies to benefit society to be missed. CSR can indeed be much more than a cost or a constraint; rather, if approached through the same frameworks that guide their core business choices, it can be a source of opportunity, innovation and competitive advantage. In order to help managers understand the strategic value of CSR, the authors outlined a new way to look at the relationship between business and society in which corporate success and social welfare are no longer intended as a zero-sum game. Their general argument is that approaching CSR strategically can become a source of great social progress. The underlying principle of this new perspective is that business and society need each other. Successful corporations need a healthy society, as it creates expanding demand for businesses and allows them to better meet human needs and growing aspirations. At the same time, a healthy society needs successful companies, as these are the most useful means to create jobs, wealth and innovation, and improve standards of living and social conditions over time. There is no social program that could work as efficiently as successful companies in fostering social development. However, the traditional approach tents to consider business and society as disparate elements, instead of recognising their points of intersection. The fact that they are mutually dependent upon each other implies that both business decisions and social policies must follow the principle of shared value, taking decisions that could benefit both sides. In fact, if adopted behaviours only benefited the interests of either business or society at the expense of each other, there could be severe consequences, as a temporary gain for one would undermine the long-term prosperity of both.

The interdependence between business and society mainly takes two forms. First, a company normally impacts upon society with its operation in the course of business, which the authors call inside-out linkages. These can have both positive and negative social consequences, and widely vary according to the location in which the company is settled, and also over time, with the evolution of social standards and scientific progress. The concept of sustainable development is largely driven from these linkages: companies should not rely on surviving by merely monitoring the social impacts of today without a careful process of identifying the evolving social effects of tomorrow.

External conditions also influence corporations in both positive and negative ways. The authors call these outside-in linkages. The competitive context in which every company operates significantly affects its ability to carry out its strategy, especially from a long-term perspective. Ensuring the health of the competitive context benefits both the company and the community. Given the importance of creating shared value for both companies and society, the measurement process takes on a key role, as it allows organizations to understand the extent to which they affect and are affected by society. Furthermore, the assessment of outcomes has a key role in unlocking new value for organizations and is important for creating opportunities for innovation and growth that would otherwise be missed (Porter et al. 2012).

3.2.3 Triple Bottom Line

The Triple Bottom Line (TBL) of social, environmental, and economic performance has garnered increasing corporate, governmental, and NGO support. The term was coined by Elkington (1997) in his book *Cannibals with Forks: The Triple Bottom Line of 21st Century Business*. With this provocative title the author seeks to find an answer to the question posed by a Polish poet: “Is it progress if a cannibal uses a fork?”, applying it to contemporary capitalism. His thesis is that progress and genuine CSR require more than the adoption of some green-washing to make over big business and/or government, supporting the need to closely focus firms’ attention on their environmental, social, and economic value (Vanclay 2004).

From this perspective, companies should be prepared in three different and separate categories that Elkington calls bottom lines. The first concerns the traditional measure of corporate profit and loss; the second is the bottom line of a company’s people account, referring to the extent to which an organization acts in a socially responsible way through its operations; and the third refers to an evaluation of how activities are carried out in an environmentally responsible way. The TBL concept thus consists of three Ps: profit, people and planet. It focuses organizations not just on the economic value they add, but also on the environmental and social value they create and destroy. Only in this way can organizations take into account the full cost involved in doing business. From a narrow perspective, the triple bottom line is used to indicate a framework for measuring and reporting corporate performance against economic, social and environmental parameters. However, in its broadest meaning it embraces the whole set of values, issues and processes that companies must address in order to minimize any harm resulting from their activities and create economic, social and environmental value. This involves being clear about the company's purpose and taking into consideration the needs of all the company's stakeholders (SustainAbility 2003). Thus, the measurement process is just a part of the whole TBL philosophy, even if it has become a key framework for accounting and reporting.

The concept of TBL has been partially criticized by Vanclay (2004), who argues that the whole concept and the role of the social within TBL are not fundamentally different to the overall field of impact assessment. Also, the concept of TBL is meant to be heuristic, a philosophy about CSR that should drive organizations' actions towards incorporating social and environmental considerations into their profit-seeking mission, though in practice great emphasis is put on identifying indicators. In the author's perspective this could lead to belittling the analysis based only on what can be counted.

TBL can indeed be seen as the sum of EIA, SIA and cost-benefit analysis, considered together in a unique framework. A notable difference is that TBL is focused at the organizational level, while SIA is usually more project-oriented.

3.2.4 Blended Value Proposition

The analysis of the investment sector is the starting point of Emerson's (2003) development of the Blended Value Proposition (BVP) concept. This features a growing awareness of the social and environmental performance of firms, not as a means for improving corporate image or advancing marketing campaign, but as a strategy for increasing the total value of companies, as well as a discussion of how the value of the non-financial performance of capital investment portfolios can be tracked.

Focusing on investment, Emerson identifies several different instruments for giving capital: grants, recoverable grants, program-related investments, loans, and market-rate loans. The differentiating element of these instruments is the type of return they seek. Instruments such as grants seek full social value with no consideration of financial performance, while instruments such as market-rate loans do not take social value into consideration and measure performance strictly on financial and economic terms. This distinction underlines how the common understanding of both investment and return is founded upon a traditional separation in the creation of social versus economic value. Emerson states that this distinction is wrong. Organizations should move beyond the traditional belief that the economic value they create is separate from and at odds with their social value;

the two are wrongly viewed as two separate aspects of the corporation's value proposition. What is in place is indeed a dynamic interplay between these components, and it happens in every organization regardless of the legal form: value itself already consists of a mix of various components. For this reason it is more correct to consider all organizations as generating a sort of "blended ROI", where value is intended as a blend of three primary elements. As Emerson explains, the main challenge is the creation of the appropriate tools that allow an organization to track and assess its performance according to this view of value.

Looking back to the analysis of the investment tools, a blending value orientation at corporate and sectorial levels assumes that the optimum investment is one that acknowledges the reality of blended economic and social value, and attempts to maximize total returns.

3.3 Defining Social Impact Assessment

3.3.1 The Meaning of Social Impact

The existing literature on this topic, both national and international, mostly focuses on the analysis of the definitions of SIA rather than on explaining what social impact means specifically. What emerges from a literature analysis is a nebulously defined approach to the investigated concepts. Even the terminology can be confusing (Nicholls 2007; Maas and Liket 2011). Social impact is the societal and environmental change created by activities and investments (Epstein and Yuthas 2014). It is described as a combination of resources, inputs, processes or policies that occurs as a result of the real, implied, or imagined presence or actions of individuals in achieving their desired outcomes (Latané 1981; Emerson et al. 2000; Reisman and Giennap 2004). As a result of externally induced actions, it includes the intended and unintended effects, the negative and positive effects, and both the long- and short-term effects (Wainwright 2002; Epstein and Yuthas 2014).

To fully understand the concept of impact, what is needed is a shift from the output perspective to the outcome perspective (Hehenberger et al. 2013). Outputs are the results that organizations can measure or assess directly, as tangible results of their activities (e.g. number of trained people, percentage of new people in the workforce), while the outcomes are the wider changes, benefits and knowledge that they attempt to elicit in the world in the medium and long term (e.g. reduction of social exclusion, decrease in inequalities). Since outcomes refer to changes in the society, they are determined by a wide range of actors as well as by external conditions that could facilitate them. Organizations can of course have a key role in driving the change, though their contributions must not be overestimated. For this reason the concept of social impact refers to the portion of the total outcome that occurred due to an organization's activities above and beyond what would have happened anyway (Clark et al. 2004).

Table 3.1 Variables of social impact

Author	Year	Variables of social impact
Armour	1990	People's way of life; culture; community
Gramling and Freudenberg	1992	Biophysical and health systems; cultural systems; social systems; political/legal systems; economic systems; psychological systems
Juslén	1995	Standard social impacts (noise level, pollution); psychosocial impacts (community cohesion, disruption of social networks); anticipatory fear; impacts of carrying out the assessment; impacts on state and private services; impacts on mobility
Vanclay	1999	People's way of life; culture; community; political system; environment; health and wellbeing; personal and property rights; fear and aspirations
Burdge	2003	Population characteristics; community and institutional structures; conflicts between local residents and newcomers; individual and family changes; community resources
Ashoka	2013	Market dynamics and value chains; public policy and industry norms; full inclusion and empathy; business-social congruence; culture of change-making

Along with defining what social impact is, scholars have specifically tried to list its constituent elements in order to provide a collection of standard variables that can be used when assessing the phenomenon. Table 3.1 shows some of the main contributions.

The need driving these attempts is that of establishing some key points that could help organizations to identify and assess social impacts. However, summarizing the potential impacts in a list of standardized indicators is problematic because the social impacts that are likely to be significant will vary from place to place and from project to project, and the weight assigned to each social impact will vary from community to community and between different groups within a given community. The debate about the appropriateness of these lists acknowledges the risk that organizations will rely on them instead of undertaking fieldwork or involving the public in determining the locally important issues; however, they can be a useful starting point for increasing organizations' awareness of the full range of social impacts that can be assessed, leading them to improved results (Vanclay 2002).

The absence of a well-defined general approach to the concept of social impact can be caused by multiple factors. Maas and Liket (2011) identified four main obstacles: (a) social impacts are often difficult to measure and quantify because of their qualitative nature, which makes it hard to link an objective value to the impact and to summarize the various qualitative expressions of impact; (b) corporations can have a positive or negative impact upon the society along several dimensions, and this can create confusion in adding up different kind of impacts; (c) social impact includes short-term as well as long-term effects on society; (d) many components can contribute to social impact, and it is often hard to link activities and impact because of difficulties with attribution and causality questions.

3.3.2 The Assessment Process

Impact assessment can be broadly defined as the prediction or estimation of the consequences of a current or proposed action (e.g. project, policy, technology). The application of this concept to the field of social impact has led to the development of an extensive body of literature in which there is no generally agreed-upon definition of the phenomenon.

SIA is one of the systems of impact management introduced to support the process of decision-making and orient it to the goal of promoting sustainable development. As it promotes the cost-effectiveness of projects in the long run, SIA has been applied to a wide range of arenas (e.g. mining, agriculture, fishery, education, supply chain management) (Wong and Ho 2015). Table 3.2 lists some of the most important definitions of SIA. These suggest that SIA can be defined as a comparative process (Burdge 2003) through which organizations can assess a broad range of impacts that are likely to be experienced by an equally broad range of social groups (Freudenburg 1986), and whose primary purpose is to enable a more sustainable and equitable biophysical and human environment (Vanclay 2003). This process allows organizations to clarify, measure and gather evidence of the benefits they create for stakeholders in the environment and the local economy; it is extremely important as a way of knowing when an activity is actually revolutionizing an industry and changing the system (Ashoka 2013). Particular emphasis is often given to the proponent- or community-led aspects of SIA, stressing that it has to be a participatory process that enables community discussions and where proposed interventions are agreed among stakeholders through negotiations. Involving stakeholders is indeed seen as a means to ensuring the equity and transparency of decision-making processes and benefiting from local knowledge (Vanclay 1999).

In these definitions, particular attention should be paid to the SIA timeframe (see Fig. 3.2). Occasionally the assessment is understood as an antecedent process aimed at helping decision-makers to decide whether the project should proceed with or without selected changes or be completely dropped, and to develop mitigation plans to overcome the potential negative impacts on individuals and communities (Interorganizational Committee on Guidelines and Principles 1994; Burdge 1999; Council For Social Development 2010). In these works, the term "assessment" takes on an unusual meaning: it is used to indicate a process that is performed before the impact actually occurs, whereas it commonly refers to an ex-post audit. In its first delineations, the concept of SIA was indeed considered as a tool to predict and mitigate the estimated social consequences of actions. However several scholars moved from this view, stating the importance of SIA also as an ex-post assessment to monitor the impact that occurs as a result of held activities, and to manage it to mitigate disadvantages and increase benefits (Vanclay 2003; Aucamp et al. 2011). Understanding SIA as a management tool allows organizations to use this process in a goal-oriented and proactive way and drive their actions to result in advantages and development for communities.

Table 3.2 Definitions of social impact assessment

Author	Year	Definition of social impact assessment
Freudenburg	1986	SIA refers to assessing (as in measuring or summarizing) a broad range of impacts (or effects, or consequences) that are likely to be experienced by an equally broad range of social groups as a result of some course of action
Interorganizational Committee on Guidelines and Principles	1994	We define SIA in terms of efforts to assess or estimate, in advance, the social consequences that are likely to follow from specific policies or actions
Branch and Ross	1997	SIA needs to be project-oriented to ensure that social issues are included in project design, planning and implementation, as well as ensuring that development is acceptable, equitable and sustainable
Goodland	2000	SIA is more than a technique or step; rather, it is a philosophy about development and democracy. As such, ideally, it considers pathologies of development, goals of development, and processes of development
Burdge	2003	The goal of SIA is to help individuals and communities, as well as government and private-sector organizations, understand and better anticipate the possible social consequences for human populations and communities of planned and unplanned social change resulting from proposed policies, plans, programs and projects
Vanclay	2003	SIA includes the process of analysing, monitoring and managing the intended and unintended social consequences, both positive and negative, of planned interventions (policy, programs, plans, projects) and any social change process invoked by those interventions
Council for social development	2010	SIA is a process that seeks to assess in advance the social repercussions that are likely to follow from projects undertaken to promote development […] As an aid to the decision-making process, SIA provides information on social and cultural factors that need to be taken into account in any decision that affects the lives of project area people
Ashoka	2013	We define impact as the system changes that result from the fellows, ideas, and networks we support
Epstein and Yuthas	2014	Social impact measurement is designed to identify changes in social impacts that result from [an organization's] activities. Most organizations measure the outputs they produce (for example, meals served or jobs created). Social impact measurement assesses the ultimate impacts of those outputs on individuals and the environment (for example the quality of life, or survival of species)

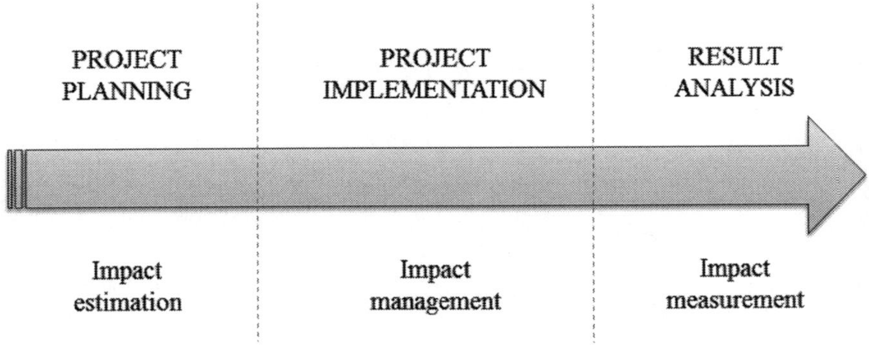

Fig. 3.2 SIA as a lifelong process

3.3.3 *The Meaning of "Social" in Social Impact Assessment: Evolving Perspectives*

This overview has presented a global vision of the theoretical framework of SIA studies. It is highly useful to understand that despite an uncertain approach to the concept, there are different perspectives according to which SIA could be studied. In particular, the meaning of the term "social" in SIA is still not clear, nor is the weight that it should have in defining the overall process. From a narrow perspective SIA refers to a portion of the TBL concept concerning societal indicators. Authors like Vanclay (2004) consider SIA as an element that has to be combined with environmental and economic impact assessment to give organizations an idea of their overall effect on society and on the surrounding area. From this perspective, the term "social" then has a narrow meaning, as it refers particularly to the assessment of those indicators that express organizations' impact on communities. As shown in Fig. 3.3, in this case, we could refer to it as "societal" impact assessment.

Fig. 3.3 Narrow perspective (TBL) of "social" in SIA

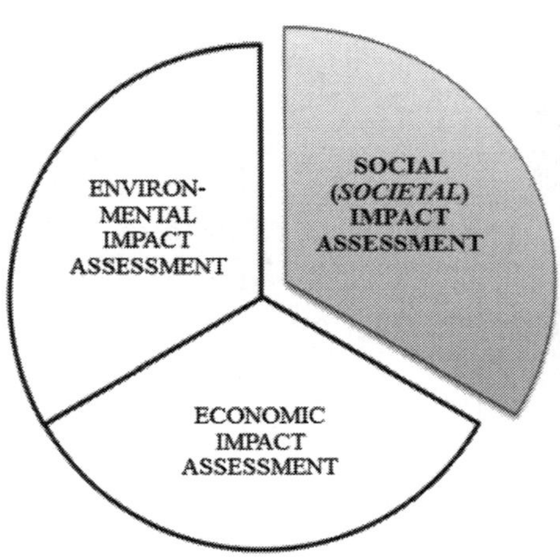

A wider perspective also exists in which the term "social" has a more general meaning and SIA is not merely considered to be part of an overall measurement process that includes environmental and economic indicators; rather, it refers to the assessment of non-economic outcomes that are more pertinent to the overall aim of the organization. From this point of view, the concept of SIA is intended as a means of building an idea of an organization's impact that goes beyond the purely economic. Here, the concept of social impact refers not only to the impact on people or communities or on goals like poverty reduction or social exclusion. Finsterbusch and Freudenburg (2002) more precisely refer to the concept of socio-economic impact assessment, which consists of a "socio-half" that can be viewed as covering social and cultural impacts of development, and an "economic-half" that includes economics, demography and planning. From this perspective, SIA concerns the need for organizations to adopt a new outlook that goes beyond the creation of profits, focusing on economic and non-economic sources of impact (see Fig. 3.4).

In order to overcome this dichotomous view, SIA can be considered as a socio-centred process in which social wellness takes on a core meaning. In the assessment process, all the different kinds of indicators are foreseen because all of them are useful means for benefiting society. Even non-profit organizations and social enterprises have, indeed, to ensure an economic sustainability in order to keep operating and growing, and to ensure sustainable development, paying attention to the surrounding environment. The difference lies in the ways these indicators are intended; from a socio-centred perspective, organizations' efforts are fully addressed to benefiting society through the fulfilment of economic and environmental, as well as societal, goals. According to this more complete view, SIA refers to a socio-centred perspective of organizations' activities in which benefiting society is the main goal. In this sense, assessing impact means evaluating economic, environmental and societal indicators to ensure the organization is really striving for society's wellbeing with all its means (see Fig. 3.5).

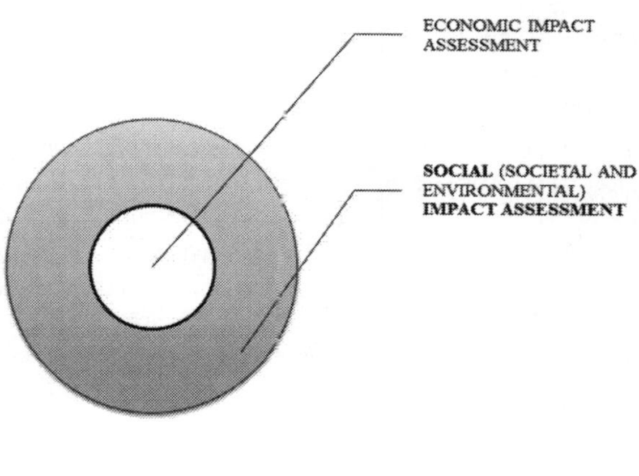

Fig. 3.4 Broad perspective of "social" in SIA

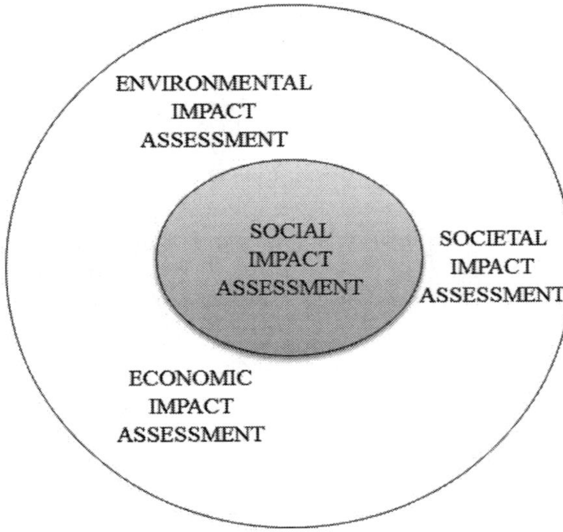

Fig. 3.5 Socio-centred perspective of SIA

3.4 "The Invisible Heart of Markets": Impact Investing and Social Impact Assessment

The need to assess social impact is also stressed by the investment sector. Witnessing the trend of using investment models to solve social needs, several tools have recently emerged. This trend is perfectly embodied by the development of impact investing. Impact investments are investments in companies, organizations and funds aimed at generating a measurable social and environmental impact, while ensuring at the same time a financial return for investors. The first definition of impact investing was coined by the Rockefeller Foundation, which in 2007 started the Global Impact Investing Network (GIIN) with around 200 investment funds. At the first Bellagio meeting in 2007, leading thinkers discussed an appropriate definition, describing impact investing as the use of profit-seeking investment to generate social and environmental good (Freireich and Fulton 2009). While the boundaries of the term remain subject to debate, subsequent attempts have sought to bring more rigour to this definition. A report co-published by J.P. Morgan, the GIIN, and the Rockefeller Foundation, released in 2010, proposes perhaps the most terse definition to date: impact investing concerns those investments intended to create a positive impact beyond financial returns. In its simplicity, this definition clearly underlines two elements that have a key role in identifying impact investing: the blend of financial and social returns, and the intention of the investment to generate both (O'Donohoe et al. 2010). Concerning the former element, impact investments actively place capital in businesses and funds that generate social and/or environmental goods, services, or benefits such as creating good jobs, with expected financial returns. As they leverage the private sector, these investments can provide solutions on a scale that purely philanthropic interventions usually cannot match. The action of an impact investor is based on the concept of additionality: beneficial social outcomes that would otherwise not occur but for investment. As impact investors are socially motivated, they intend to achieve social goals. Thus the main issue is to understand whether or not an investment actually has a social impact.

Concerning the second element, the intention of impact investment vehicles to make a social/environmental impact is a primary qualifying criterion; investments that unintentionally result in social good are not regarded as impact investments. For this reason impact investment is different from socially responsible investment (SRI), which is based on negative screening to avoid investing in harmful companies, or on shareholder activism to encourage CSR practices (Freireich and Fulton 2009). Having impact implies causation, and therefore depends on the idea of the counterfactual—what would have happened if a particular investment or activity had not occurred. The goal of these investments is achieved only if they produce social outcomes that would not otherwise have occurred (Brest and Born 2013).

Impact investing was born and firstly developed in Anglo-Saxon markets, where it has reached a more developed level than in countries like Italy, where many tools are at their embryonic stage. In the US, for example, the development of this phenomenon has been due to a strategic repositioning of several philanthropic foundations that, because of the financial crisis, have renewed their strategies and strongly supported the launch of impact investment practices. In the UK, impact investing depends on the institutional activity that, from 2000 with Tony Blair, led to a structured environment whose pivot is Big Society Capital, a financial intermediary founded by public funds and the private banking sector. In their first form impact investments were mostly intended to support social businesses in developing countries, to meet the needs of people in the so-called "Bottom of the Pyramid[1]". In these contexts the aim of impact investments is quite different, as their main purpose is to ensure basilar services (e.g. health, water, education, energy efficiency) to the whole population. However, even in advanced economies social inclusion is becoming an important issue that requires strong interventions (Social Impact Investing Taskforce 2014).

In recent years there has been a convergence of factors that have pushed forward the concept and practice of impact investing. Harji and Jackson (2012) identified those drivers that have generated new interest and activity in impact investing:

- The financial crisis has revealed the limitations of traditional models of investment decision-making and risk assessment, boosting the integration of environmental, social and governance factors into investment decisions.

[1] The concept of "Bottom of the Pyramid" refers to those segments of a population that live on less than £2.50 per day. (For further information see Prahalad (2004), *Fortune at the Bottom of the Pyramid,* Wharton School Publishing).

- As the scale of social and environmental challenges continues to grow, there is increasing awareness that the existing set of resources allocated to addressing these issues is insufficient, as well as a stronger desire to supplement both philanthropy and public money in addressing these challenges.
- An emerging set of activities and investments is demonstrating the sustainable and scalable returns of business models deliberately generating blended value.
- New generations of professionals are growing with the principle of seeking money and meaning, nurturing the trend of embedding social values into their investing activities.

The cumulative effect of these factors has been to give a significant boost to the organization and growth of the impact-investing industry. It goes without saying that SIA takes on an unavoidable key role, as social outcomes are the main aim of these investment tools. Moreover, most of these forms of investment make payment conditional upon success; thus the need for a validation of the achievement of the agreed goals is directly linked to the remuneration of investors.

Table 3.3 lists some examples of impact-investing tools that are result-based, raising the issue of measuring social outcome. Usually techniques to measure social outcomes are defined each time on the basis of the project. However, the lack of standardized practices to assess goal achievement could severely hamper the further development of these innovative sources of funding, from which social enterprises could widely benefit.

Table 3.3 Examples of impact investing tools

Instrument	Description
Social impact bond	This is an agreement between one or more government agencies and external organizations where the government specifies one or more outcomes and promises to pay the external organization a pre-agreed sum if it is able to accomplish the outcome. The offered sum can be paid only if the investor achieves that goal
Development impact bond	This works like social impact bonds. A distinguishing feature is that external agencies are involved in providing the outcome payment (or some portion of it), in partnership with a developing country's government
Cash on delivery aid	Donors agree to pay the recipient government a fixed amount for incremental progress made towards a predefined outcome that is independently verified before payments are made
Microfinance	This involves providing financial products to small businesses run by people in disadvantaged groups, giving them the opportunity to become financially self-sufficient
Green bonds	These are capital-raising instruments specifically for projects with positive environmental benefits

Adapted from Centre for Social Development and Social Finance (2013); RBC Social Finance (2014)

Box 3.1: Social Impact Bonds, theory and practice

Social Impact Bonds (SIBs) are a remarkable example of how tools belonging to traditional finance can be reshaped to meet a social purpose, as they are based on a novel government-funding structure that focuses on funding outcomes rather than on funding inputs into government programs. A SIB is an agreement between one or more government agencies and external organizations where the government specifies one or more outcomes and promises to pay the external organization a pre-agreed sum if it is able to accomplish the outcome (Kohli et al. 2012). The offered sum can be paid only if the investor achieves that goal. In this sense, the term "bond" is misleading because bonds generally offer a fixed rate of return. Conversely, SIBs are likely riskier investments because the external organization receives a return only if certain outcomes are met.

SIBs may be structured in different ways, but all of them share similar features in terms of the actors involved: the government agencies to define a desired outcome; an external organization to execute the programs that deliver the outcome, often known as a service provider; and a population that benefits from the services. Additionally, even if they are not necessary, most SIBs involve investors who provide seed capital to fund the external organization's activities, as well as intermediaries who manage the overall SIB project. Evaluation advisers can also be included to help monitor and redefine the program, and independent assessors to determine if the SIB targets are met.

There are several benefits of SIBs that make them more advantageous then traditional forms of government funding. First, SIBs tie profit to socially valuable results. By avoiding the need to finance a project with taxpayers' money, SIBs transfer the risk from the government to either the investors who provide initial capital, or the external organization. In fact, the government compensates the investors or external organization only if the target outcomes are met (Callanan et al. 2012). This is an important benefit as it mitigates wasteful public spending while also incentivizing organizations to target programs that achieve results. Also, SIBs provide seed capital to programs that lack funding because of limited government revenue due to the 2008 recession. Finally, SIBs enable collaboration among different actors in the public and private sectors, allowing each actor to execute the portion of the project in which it excels (Baliga 2013).

The first SIB was developed and launched in the UK in 2010. To fund it, Social Finance UK, a non-profit organization supported by 17 foundations, raised £5 million in seed capital from investors. The social outcome it aims to achieve is to help 3000 short-term male prisoners at Peterborough (divided into three cohorts of 1000) stay out of prison once they are released, supporting them in building a new life outside. To this end Social Finance set up a new service known as the One Service, which includes as delivery organizations the St Giles Trust, Sova, Ormiston Families, YMCA and MIND in order to provide housing, family, healthcare, and employment and training support. The quantitative indicator for this outcome is the reduction of the recidivist rate against a control group: if there is at least a 10 % reduction in reoffending per cohort or a 7.5 % reduction across all cohorts, the investors will receive a payment; the greater the reduction, the higher the return to investors (max. 13 % per year). Being a pay-for-success type of investment, if the reduction is lower than the established threshold, investors have effectively made a philanthropic donation, as they will not get their money back.

The results of the first cohort were released in August 2014 and demonstrated an 8.4 % reduction in the reconviction rate relative to the comparable national baseline. Although a reduction of 10 % was needed for an immediate repayment to investors, if the reduction in reoffending remains above 7.5 %, investors are on track to receive a positive return in 2016.

3.5 Mapping the Practice of Social Impact Assessment in Social Enterprises

The practice of SIA is particularly useful for social enterprises that have a need to assess the value of their activity beyond the economic and financial output. Quantitative studies on the implementation of SIA processes are not numerous. Just as for SE, it is not easy to empirically analyse the practice of SIA using quantitative methods; case studies may therefore be a better way of capturing the complexity of this phenomenon. However, some attempts to map the diffusion of SIA within social enterprises have been made in order to increase knowledge of developments in the field and verify whether or not some general trends are identifiable. At a global level, an interesting contribution comes from the Global Entrepreneurship Monitor (GEM)[2]; a question on impact assessment was indeed included in the survey. Although impact assessment was not considered to be one of the elements that should univocally define social enterprises, its inclusion was foreseen because several researchers consider SIA to be a fundamental differentiator between social enterprises and more traditional forms of social activity. It is also recognized as a key element in gauging the real impact of SE and its effectiveness in healing the world's problems (Lepoutre et al. 2013).

Respondents were questioned about intentions and actual practices related to impact measurements. This question was also the basis of a study by Grieco and Maas (2014). Starting from the GEM dataset, they developed a logistic regression model to assess the extent to which some of the organizations' features can be considered as influencing social entrepreneurs' willingness to measure the

[2] See Sect. 2.5.

generated impact. In particular, considering the question on impact assessment as the dependent variable, they tested how it is influenced by social mission, market orientation and innovativeness. They controlled the model according to age and size of social enterprise.

As summarized in Table 3.4, the output of this research is important as it provides a quantitative analysis of the behaviour of social entrepreneurs in approaching SIA, and allows some general conclusions about their lines of action to be drawn.

What emerges is that the willingness to assess social impact is positively associated with the level of innovativeness and the size of the organization, while a negative association is discernible between SIA and the importance given to social goals and the exposure to market trends

The positive associations are confirmations of the driving role of assessing impact to foster innovation (Nicholls 2007), and of institutional theory and

Table 3.4 Results summarized

Variable	GEM question	Effect on impact measurement
Social value	Organizations may have goals according to their ability to generate economic value, societal value and environmental value. Please allocate a total of 100 points across these three categories as they pertain to your goals	Negative: the more social enterprises give points to social mission, the less they assess impact
Innovativeness	Is your activity, organization or initiative offering a new type of product or service?	Positive: the more social enterprises claim to be innovative, the more they assess impact
	Is your activity, organization or initiative offering a new way of producing a product or service?	
	Is your activity, organization or initiative offering a new way of delivering a product or service?	
	Is your activity, organization or initiative offering a new way of promoting or marketing a product or service?	
	Is your activity, organization or initiative attending a new or so far unattended market niche or customer?	
Market orientation	What percentage of total income comes from the sale of products or services?	Negative: the more social enterprises are market oriented, the less they assess impact
Age	What was the first year the activity, organization or initiative provided services to others, or received external funding? Specification of year	None: no significant effects are discernible from the study
Size	Right now how many people, not counting the owners but including subcontractors, part-time workers and volunteers, are working for this activity, organization or initiative? Number of employees	Positive: the larger the social enterprise, the more it assesses impact

accounting literature stating that large organizations are more subject to legitimacy concerns and more willing to use sophisticated accounting methods (Cinquini and Tenucci 2007). More surprising is that striving for social goals is not positively associated with impact measurement. The authors suggest several reasons for this, including the newness of SIA as a field of analysis and the warm-glow feeling of working in the non-profit sector (Andreoni 1990; Donegani et al. 2012). In line with previous scholars (Baron 2007; Hoogendoorn 2011), this result seems to show that the warm-glow feeling of aiming for social value is stronger than the need for validation of expectations. Finally, for those who are less market-oriented, the practice of impact measurement is more widespread probably because of the higher importance those entrepreneurs give to other kinds of revenues, like donations and loans, that require them to be accountable in a different way. However, competing on the market does not seem to encourage the need for disclosure of this kind of information.

The age of social enterprises does not seem to have any effect on their willingness to implement SIA processes. Kramer's analysis (2005) underlines the relation between life cycle stage and the necessity of measuring social impact. What emerges from the interviews he administered is that those funders who focus on the earliest stages do not necessarily expect the SEs to be cost-effective. Therefore, they do not really rely on the evaluation of the efficiency of outcomes or on the degree of impact at this early stage. It could also be assumed that since social impact is mainly focused on the long term, nascent SEs do not have a complete view of the actual impact that their activities have on society. SIA is a relatively new field of inquiry, however, so it is reasonable to assume that organizations that have been founded more recently will be more aware of opportunities and the need to measure impact.

References

Armour, A. (1990). Integrating impact assessment in the planning process: From rhetoric to reality. *Impact Assessment, 8*(1–2), 1–14.

Ashoka. (2013). How do you know when you've revolutionized an industry? Ashoka's approach to assessing impact. https://www.ashoka.org/files/2013-Impact-Study-FINAL-web.pdf.

Andreoni, J. (1990). Impure altruism and donations to public goods: A theory of warm-glow giving. *The Economic Journal, 100*(401), 464–477.

Aucamp, I. C., Woodborne, S., Perold, J. J., Bron, A., & Aucamp, S. M. (2011). Looking beyond impact assessment to social sustainability. New directions in social impact assessment: Conceptual and methodological advances, pp. 38–58.

Bagnoli, L., & Megali, C. (2011). Measuring performance in social enterprises. *Non-profit and Voluntary Sector Quarterly, 40*(1), 149–165.

Baliga, S. (2013). Shaping the success of social impact bonds in the United States: Lessons learned from the privatization of US prisons. *Duke LJ, 63*, 437.

Baron, R. A. (2007). Behavioral and cognitive factors in entrepreneurship: Entrepreneurs as the active element in new venture creation. *Strategic Entrepreneurship Journal, 1*(1–2), 167–182.

Brest, P., & Born, K. (2013). When can impact investing create real impact? *Stanford Social Innovation Review, 11*, 22–27.

Brown, J., & Fraser, M. (2006). Approaches and perspectives in social and environmental accounting: an overview of the conceptual landscape. *Business Strategy and the Environment, 15*, 103–117.

Brown, L., & Moore, M. (2001). 2001. *Accountability, strategy, and international nongovernmental organizations, non-profit and voluntary sector quarterly, 30*, 569.

Burdge, J. (1999). A community guide to social impact assessment, Reviewed edition, Social Economy Press.

Burdge, R. J. (2003). The practice of social impact assessment—background. *Impact Assessment and Project Appraisal 21*(2), 84–88.

Burton, B. K., & Dunn, C. P. (1996). Feminist ethics as moral grounding for stakeholder theory. *Business Ethics Quarterly, 6*, 133–147.

Callanan, L., Law, J., & Mendonca, L., (2012). From potential to action: Bringing social impact bonds to US. New York: Mc Kinsey & Company.

Centre for Social Development and Social Finance. (2013). Investing in social outcomes: Development impact bonds the report of the development impact bond working group. http://www.cgdev.org/sites/default/files/investing-in-social-outcomes-development-impact-bonds.pdf.

Cinquini, L., Tenucci, A. (2007). Is the adoption of strategic management accounting techniques really 'strategy-driven'? Evidence from a survey. Available at SSRN http://ssrn.com/abstract=1012881.

Clark, C., Rosenzweig, W., Long, D., & Olsen, S. (2004). Double bottom line project report: Assessing social impact in double bottom line ventures. http://www.riseproject.org/DBL_Methods_Catalog.pdf.

Council for social development. (2010). *Social impact assessment*, Report of a research project on social impact assessment of R&R policies and packages in India, New Delhi.

Cutt, J., & Murray, V. (2002). Accountability and effectiveness evaluation in non-profit organizations. London: Routledge.

Deegan, C. (2002). Introduction—the legitimising effect of social and environmental disclosures—a theoretical foundation. *Accounting, Auditing and Accountability Journal, 15*(3), 282–311.

Dierkes, M., & Antal, A. B. (1986). Whither corporate social reporting: Is it time to legislate? *California Management Review, XXVIII*(3), 106–121.

Donegani, C. P., McKay, S., & Moro, D. (2012). A dimming of the 'warm glow'? are non-profit workers in the UK still more satisfied with their jobs than other workers? *Advances in the Economic Analysis of Participatory and Labor-Managed Firms, 13*, 313–342.

Ebrahim, A. S., & Rangan, V. K. (2010). The limits of non-profit impact: A contingency framework for measuring social performance. Harvard Business School General Management Unit Working Paper, pp. 10–099.

Ebrahim, A., & Weisband, E. (2007). Global accountabilities: Participation, pluralism and public ethics (Vol. 23, pp. 13–28). UK: Cambridge University Press.

Elkington, J. (1997). *Cannibals with forks: The triple bottom line of 21st century business.* Oxford: Capstone.

Emerson, J. (2003). The blended value preposition: Integrating social and financial return. *California Management Review, 45*(4), 35–51.

Emerson, J., Wachowics, J., & Chun, S. (2000). *Social return on investment: Exploring aspects of value creation in the non-profit sector.* San Francisco: The Roberts Foundation.

Epstein, M. J., & Yuthas, K. (2014). Measuring and improving social impacts: A guide for non-profits, companies, and impact investors; BK Business.

Epstein, M., Flamholtz, E., & McDonough, J. J. (1976). Corporate social accounting in the United States of America: state of the art and future prospects. *Accounting, Organizations and Society, 1*(1), 23–42.

Finsterbusch, K., & Freudenburg, W. R. (2002). Social impact assessment and technology assessment. In R. E. Dunlap & W. E. Michelson (Eds.), *Handbook of environmental sociology* (pp. 407–447). Westport, Conn: Greenwood Press.

Freireich, J., & Fulton, K. (2009). Investing for social and environmental impact: A design for catalyzing an emerging industry. US: The Monitor Group.

Freudenburg, W. R. (1986). Social impact assessment. *Annual Review of Sociology, 12*, 451–478.

Goodland, R. (2000). Social and environmental assessment to promote sustainability: An informal view from the World Bank. Environment Department Paers Nr. 74, Washington, DC: The World Bank.

Gramling, R., & Freudenburg, W. R. (1992). Opportunity-threat, development, and adaptation: Toward a comprehensive framework for social impact assessment. *Rural Sociology, 57*(2), 216–234.

Gray, R. H., Owen, D. L., & Adams, C. A. (1996). *Accounting and accountability: Changes and challenges in corporate social and environmental reporting*. Hemel Hempstead: Prentice Hall.

Grieco, C., & Maas, K. (2014). Mapping the practice of social impact assessment: A quantitative study on social enterprises, EMAN conference proceedings, Rotterdam, March 27–28, 2014.

Harji, K., & Jackson, E. T. (2012). Accelerating impact. achievements, challenges and what's next in building the impact investing industry. New York City: The Rockefeller Foundation.

Hehenberger, L., Harling, A.M., & Scholten, P. (2013). A practical guide to measuring and managing impact. Belgium: European Venture Philanthropy Association.

Hildebrandt, L., & Sandham, L. A. (2014). Social impact assessment: The lesser sibling in the South African EIA process? *Environmental Impact Assessment Review, 48*, 20–26.

Hoogendoorn, B. (2011). Social entrepreneurship in the modern economy: Warm glow, cold feet. Netherlands: Erasmus University Rotterdam.

Interorganizational Committee on Guidelines and Principles for Social Impact Assessment. (1994). Guidelines and principles for social impact assessment. *Impact Assessment, 12*(2), 107–152.

Juslén, J. (1995). Social impact assessment: A look at finnish experiences. *Project Appraisal, 10* (3), 163–170.

Kohli, J., Besharov, D. J., & Costa, K. (2012). Social impact bonds 101. Defining an innovative new financing tool for social programs. Washington, DC: Center for American Progress.

Kolk, A. (2005). Sustainability reporting. *Vba Journal nr, 3*, 2005.

Kramer, M. R. (2005). Measuring innovation: Evaluation in the field of social entrepreneurship, Foundation Strategy Group.

Latanè, B. (1981). The psychology of social impact. *American Psychologist, 36*(4), 343–356.

Le Ber, M., Bansal, P., & Branzei, O. (2010). Managing the tensions between social and economic value in hybrid organizations, conference proceedings A.S.A.C. 2010 Enterprising our world, sustainable business in action, 22–25th May, Regina (Sk).

Lepoutre, J., Justo, R., Terjesen, S., & Bosma, N. (2013). Designing a global standardized methodology for measuring social entrepreneurship activity: The global entrepreneurship monitor social entrepreneurship study. *Small Business Economics, 40*(3), 693–714.

Maas, K., & Liket, K. (2011). Social impact measurement: Classification of methods. In Burritt, R., Schaltegger, S., Bennett, M., Pohjola, T., Csutora, M. (Eds.), Environmental management accounting and supply chain management, eco-efficiency in industry and science (Vol. 27, pp. 171–202).

Nicholls, J. (2007). Why measuring and communicating social value can help social enterprise become more competitive. Cabinet Office, Office of the Third Sector. http://evpa.eu.com/wp-content/uploads/2010/09/Why-measuring-and-communicating-social-value-can-help-social-enterprise-become-more-competitive1.pdf.

O'Donohoe, N., Leijonhufvud, C., Saltuk, Y., Bugg-Levine, A., & Brandenburg, M. (2010). Impact investments: An emerging asset class. *JP Morgan, 6*.

Perrini, F., Russo, A., & Tencati, A. (2007). CSR strategies of SMEs and large firms. Evidence from Italy. *Journal of Business Ethics, 74*(3), 285–300.

Porter, M. (1980). *Competitive Strategy*. New York: Free Press.

Porter, M. E., Hills, G., Pfitzer, M., Patscheke, S., Hawkins, E. (2012). Measuring shared value how to unlock value by linking social and business results, FSG. http://www.fsg.org/Portals/0/Uploads/Documents/PDF/Measuring_Shared_Value.pdf. Accessed May 15, 2012.

Porter, M. E., & Kramer, M. R. (2011). Creating shared value. *Harvard Business Review*, 62–77.

Porter, M. E., & Kramer, M. R. (2006). Strategy and society. *Harvard Business Review, 84*(12), 78–92.

Post, J., Preston, L., & Sachs, S. (2002). *Redefining the corporation: Stakeholder management and organisational wealth.* Palo Alto: Stanford University Press.

Prahalad, C. K. (2004). The fortune at the bottom of the pyramid: Eradicating poverty through profits.

RBC Social Finance. (2014). Financing social good: A primer on impact investing in Canada, http://www.rbc.com/community-sustainability/_assets-custom/pdf/Financing-Social-Good.pdf.

Reisman, J., & Giennap, A. (2004). Theory of change: A practical tool for action, results and learning, organizational research services. Erasmus University Rotterdam. http://www.erim.eur.nl/portal/page/portal/ERIM/Research/Centres/Erasmus_Centre_for_Strategic_Philanthropy/Research/Publications/Social_Impact_Measurement_voor_sso_nieuwsbrief%5B1%5D.pdf.

Richmond, B. J, Mook, L., & Quarter, J. (2003) Social accounting for non profits. Two models. *Non-profit Management and Leadership, 13*(4).

Sawhill, J. C., & Williamson, D. (2001). Mission impossible?: Measuring success in non-profit organizations. *Non-profit Management and Leadership, 11*(3), 371–386.

Social Impact Investing Taskforce. (2014). La finanza che include: gli investimenti ad impatto sociale per una nuova economia, Rapporto italiano della social impact investment task force istituita in ambito g8.

SustainAbility. (2003). The triple bottom line http://www.sustainability.com/philosophy/triple-bottom/tbl-intro.asp.

Vanclay, F. (1999). Social impact assessment. In Petts, J (Eds.) Handbook of environmental impact assessment, Vol. 1, pp. 301–326. Oxford: Blackwell Science.

Vanclay, F. (2002). Conceptualising social impacts. *Environmental Impact Assessment Review, 22* (3), 183–211.

Vanclay, F. (2003). International principles for social impact assessment. *Impact Assessment and Project Appraisal, 21*(1), 5–11.

Vanclay, F. (2004). The triple bottom line and impact assessment: How do tbl, eia, sia, sea and ems relate to each other? *Journal of Environmental Assessment Policy and Management, 6*(3), 265–288.

Wainwright, S. (2002). *Measuring impact: A guide to resources.* NCVO Publications, London.

Wong, C. H., & Ho, W. C. (2015). Roles of social impact assessment practitioners. *Environmental Impact Assessment Review, 50*, 124–133.

Chapter 4
How to Drive the Process?

Addressing the Landscape of Social Impact Assessment Models

Abstract This chapter presents an in-depth analysis of the wide landscape of existing models that social entrepreneurs can rely upon when approaching the SIA process. Two famous models are described, illustrating the principles on which they were developed and the indicators they use to guide the assessment process. The practice of monetization, which has been growing in popularity, is discussed, and its benefits and drawbacks described. A taxonomy is proposed to offer an attempt at classification that can help social entrepreneurs to address the great number of models available, followed by a description of the main features of four groups of SIA models. Finally, self-assessment is proposed to guide social entrepreneurs in selecting the group of models that best meets the specific needs of their organizations.

Keywords Social impact assessment · Models · SROI · Social balanced scorecard · Monetization · Self-assessment

4.1 Where to Start? The "Outcome Pathway" to Change

Interest in the practice of SIA is growing in both the academic and the practical spheres. Once the importance of this information has been understood and shared amongst actors, the need to find a way to track organizations' progress towards the achievement of social outcomes raises questions about how this can be done practically. It has been stated that measuring social impact is a case-specific action (Vanclay 2003), and that drafting guidelines may be useful; but it is impossible to prescribe in a detailed way how SIA should be carried out, as it largely depends on several specific factors such as the project to assess, the features of the organization, the external conditions, and the stakeholders. In such detailed scenarios, generally defined standards for the assessment of social impacts might risk devaluing the specificity of each case. Nevertheless, it is also true that one of the aims of SIA is to communicate results to the external stakeholders. As aforementioned, this kind of information can be highly useful to access innovative sources of funding and to justify to the investors the ways in which the resources they have provided have been used for the achievement of the declared social mission. Information about

C. Grieco, *Assessing Social Impact of Social Enterprises*,
SpringerBriefs in Business, DOI 10.1007/978-3-319-15314-8_4

social impact must always be understandable, must sometimes be comparable with other data, and of course must be collected and disclosed in a clear and consistent way, so that the recipients can be sure of its validity and reliability. This is even more important when this information is linked to a benefit (e.g. impact investing) or when it is used as a criterion for the evaluation of two or more organizations. Furthermore, the search for a shared practice of measuring and assessing social impact is beneficial for the creation of a common language that enhances the dialogue among social enterprises within different sectors (Perrini and Vurro 2013).

All of these factors prove the need for some form of standard process that could orient managers in assessing social impacts and ensure the validity of methods and results. Financial indicators and for-profit companies' standards have long been the only tools available, but their focus on economic performance makes them unsuitable for those organizations that need to assess the creation of social value. Financial measures cannot be the primary indicators of the performance of social enterprises, even if many difficulties emerge from conceptualizing and measuring the achievement of social missions. Despite these difficulties, however, efforts have been made to develop brand-new models, and to adapt existing ones, in order to focus on capturing the non-economic results of organizations.

Existing approaches range from guidelines for driving the overall process to models listing the specific indicators that should be assessed. The core idea behind all of them is the need to start from the social mission in order to define the object of the assessment and the proper indicators to verify its achievement. The specific contribution of a social enterprise can be expressed through the definition of a theory of change, which is the starting point of each measurement process. Clarifying the theory of change allows the definition of all the building blocks required for planning long-term interventions: the available resources, the input that each resource gives, the implemented activities, the resulting output, and the planned outcomes both in the short and long term. In drafting the theory of change, these elements are identified in reverse order, starting from the outcomes that the social enterprise wants to achieve, and tying them back to the output, activities, input and resources needed, in order to identify their necessary preconditions.

The process of change-making is thus drafted with causal linkages, mapped to form the "outcomes pathway". The purpose of this process is to map out how an organization's social mission will be achieved, so this can be kept in mind while activities are being planned. It is possible to say, then, that the outcome pathway is a two-way process (see Fig. 4.1). It goes from resources to outcome in its implementation, as each resource implies an input, while the input allows the development of the activities that will result in short-term output and longer-term outcomes. But the inverse also occurs when actions are planned: the social mission that the organization aims to achieve is the starting point in defining the short-term and tangible outputs from which it can derive, that are in turn the results of some activities that requires specific input and resources.

Once the mission is clear, and the ways to achieve it are established, the entrepreneur can identify the best way to assess the impact of the proposed activities and to verify the alignment of the goals.

Fig. 4.1 The two-way process of the outcome-pathway

SIA can be carried out in several ways. Many models have been developed to drive the actions of those who want to implement this process, and the wide range of choices can generate confusion among users. The following section will provide an in-depth analysis of the steps to take, and the guidelines that are generally applicable when assessing social impact, as well as specific models of their purposes and methodologies.

4.2 Running the Processes: Steps and Principles

Despite the existing models developed to assess social impact, general guidelines on how the overall process should be set up and developed have long been lacking. The very definitions of social impact and SIA can give information about what these concepts mean, but they do not say much about the practical steps to follow. The demand for certain types of guidelines on conducting SIA has grown mainly because an assessment of social impacts is often required prior to the commencement of a new project or the expansion of an existing project—though the appropriate guidelines for this purpose do not yet exist (Council for Social Development 2010). To this end, an important attempt is the *Guidelines and Principles for Social Impact Assessment* edited by the US Interorganizational Committee on Guidelines and Principles for Social Impact Assessment (1994). This publication is a milestone because it represents an agreement on the core procedures for a better understanding of the overall process of SIA. The starting point of the document is the fact that the practice of SIA was not perceived as being well-integrated into decision-making processes, probably because of its complexity or the political consequences of making explicit the social impact of projects and programs (*ibid*). Thus, the definition of a set of guidelines and principles aims to assist agencies and other institutions in implementing SIA, based on the core belief that its integration can generate better decisions. This document includes the steps to follow in implementing SIA processes, and a set of principles on which the overall process should be based.

The steps can be summarized as follows:

1. Involve all the relevant public: identify and work with all the people affected by the activities of the organization.
2. Identify alternatives: planned interventions should be listed along with reasonable alternatives.

3. Baseline conditions: describe the existing situation and any past trends associated with the environment in which the activities are going to be developed.
4. Identify the full range of impacts that could emerge (in terms of duration, probability, number of affected people, benefits and costs).
5. Investigate probable impacts.
6. Establish responses to the estimated impacts.
7. Identify indirect and cumulative impacts.
8. Draft alternatives and estimate the possible new results.
9. Develop mitigation plans to reduce adverse impacts.
10. Develop a monitoring program to gather evidence of any deviation from initial plans.

Along with these steps, nine principles are identified (see Table 4.1) to orient actions during the overall process and work as a benchmark for conducting SIA.

This document includes basic indications on the development of the process that have been widely shared and reworked by scholars (SEEE 2010; Hehenberger et al. 2013; Epstein and Yuthas 2014). Across all these works, the underlying principle is that implementing a SIA process can require different levels of detail or different operating methods, but generally it always follows a set of macro-phases (see Fig. 4.2) that could be summarized as:

Table 4.1 Principles for social impact assessment (adapted by Interorganizational Committee on Guidelines and Principles for Social Impact Assessment 1994)

Principle	Description
1. Involve the diverse public	Identify and involve all potentially affected groups and individuals
2. Analyse impact equity	Clearly identify who will win and who will lose and emphasize vulnerability of under-represented groups
3. Focus the assessment	Deal with issues and public concerns that really count, not those that are just easy to count
4. Identify methods and assumptions and define significance	Describe how the SIA is conducted, what assumptions are used and how significance is determined
5. Provide feedback on social impacts to project planners	Identify problems that could be solved with changes to the proposed action or alternatives
6. Use SIA practitioners	Trained social scientists employing social science methods will provide the best results
7. Establish monitoring and mitigation programs	Manage uncertainty by monitoring and mitigating adverse impacts
8. Identify data sources	Use published scientific literature, secondary data and primary data from the affected area
9. Plan for gaps in data	Evaluate the missing information, and develop a strategy for proceeding

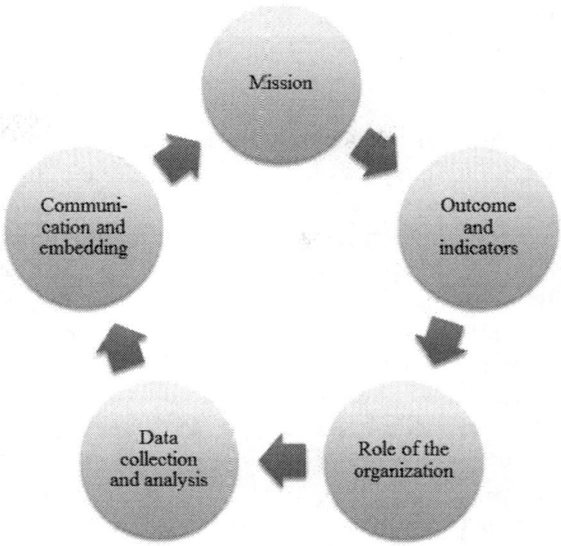

Fig. 4.2 The stages of the social impact assessment process

- identification of objective, mission, goals to achieve;
- definition of outcome and indicators;
- identification of the effective role of the organization in fulfilling outcomes;
- data collection and analysis;
- communication of the results and knowledge embedding.

These identified stages are the starting point for the development of specific models that prescribe in more detail a framework of analysis, or quantitative calculations to provide a specific measure that can be communicated in numbers. These models can be quite different from each other; although scholars are quite in agreement about the general steps of SIA process, there is less of a consensus concerning the specific models for identifying and measuring impact (Lockie 2001). The existing models are not, however, in complete opposition. Rather, they are different ways to approach the different issues involved in the impact evaluation process.

4.3 A Wide Range of Social Impact Assessment Models

4.3.1 An Overview

The growing relevance of SIA has, over time, guided the development of a multitude of different models, as many interested parties have been involved. Scholars' contributions have been numerous, along with those who illustrate newly developed models (Sawhill and Williamson 2001; Bloom and Chatterji 2009; Esteves and Vanclay 2009). There are many others whose works have been aimed at analysing models or indicators developed by non-profit organisations, universities and research centres, consulting companies and other institutions (Emerson 2003; Richmond et al. 2003; Rockefeller Foundation 2003; Hart and Haughton 2007; Boyer et al. 2008; Antonaras et al. 2011; West Sussex County Council 2011). Indeed, academics are not the only people who have demonstrated an interest in improving SIA practice. Other interested parties include SIA practitioners as well as regulatory agencies, policy and program developers, financiers and, above all, the affected people and non-profit organizations. Measurement models thus originate not only from the academic literature but also from intergovernmental organizational standards (such as the UN Global Compact, many ILO conventions and declarations, OECD guidelines, UN Principles for Responsible Investment), multilateral financial institution standards, multi-stakeholder initiative standards, industry associations, and individual company codes of practice (Vanclay 2003).

These interested parties have also developed databases of SIA models. Relevant examples come from online initiatives such as the Tools and Resources for Assessing Social Impact (TRASI) project and the New Economics Foundation (NEF). The former was launched in 2010 from the Foundation Centre (an association of more than 500 foundations worldwide) to create a database of evaluation models that currently includes more than 150 items. These models range from performance evaluation to internal audit, and include tools for the assessment of public policies as well as introduced changes within the organization. Moreover, the Foundation manages a network of non-profit organizations, financiers and social enterprises aimed at enhancing the sharing of experience. Similarly, NEF is the UK's leading think tank, working with the mission of transforming the economy and making it work both for people and the planet. In 2005 NEF published a toolkit named "Proving and Improving[1]" (updated in 2009), to provide social enterprises and other social organizations with knowledge, tools and resources to improve the quality of their activities and their impact. The toolkit includes 20 models to assess the impact, and practical indications for how to compare and chose among them.

From the organization's perspective, this proliferation necessitates the task of choosing the most suitable model according to the purpose and target of the measurement process (Perrini and Vurro 2013). There are a number of reasons for the unsuitableness of a single model that can be adapted by all organizations in the same way. First, as mentioned previously, the concept of social impact could refer to different dimensions (intended/unintended, positive/negative, short/long term), and every organization has its own interest in assessing the dimensions about which it cares most. Then, differences in size, activities, purposes, and available resources require organizations to choose a model that can somehow be tailored to these particular features. Non-profit organizations and social enterprises, in particular, also have many different stakeholders to whom they must account, and each of them can be interested in different kinds of impact.

[1] For more information please visit: http://www.neweconomics.org/publications/entry/proving-and-improving1.

Two models are among the most frequently cited in the literature and used by social enterprises: the Social Return On Investment (SROI) and the Social Balanced Scorecard (SBSC). Despite fulfilling the same purpose, the analysis of these models underlines the variety that can exist among different approaches. The SROI is a quantitative model based on the principle of monetizing impact, while the SBSC is a more general scheme of analysis that helps organizations by suggesting what they should consider when assessing social impact. The features of these two models are perfect illustrations of Zappalà and Lyons' (2009) distinction between methods and frameworks. Methods such as SROI are models that aim to provide organizations with proper indicators, often based on financial proxies. The output is a quantification of the generated impact in monetary terms. In contrast, frameworks provide a structure for organizations to think about, design, plan, implement and embed performance measurements into a project, program or organization as a whole, though they do not prescribe a particular method or specific indicators to use in assessing social impact.

This is an important distinction to keep in mind when selecting which model to implement. Methods can be more resource-consuming, the process can be longer, and financial proxies are often hard to identify; however, expressing the generated impact in terms of money makes it easier for stakeholders to understand and comparable with the results of other organizations. In contrast, frameworks do not provide social entrepreneurs with quantitative data on the generated impact, but they are often easy to apply and consume fewer resources. Also, they allow an overall view of the whole organization's activities, making it easier for them to gain an idea of the bigger picture.

4.3.2 Social Return on Investment

The Social Return On Investment (SROI) is one of the most investigated methods in the SIA literature (Emerson 2003; Lingane and Olsen 2004; Hart and Haughton 2007; Boyer et al. 2008; Olsen and Galimidi 2009a, b; Maas and Liket 2011; Perrini and Vurro 2013). It was developed by the Roberts Enterprise Development Funds (REDF), an American venture philanthropy organization that aims to propose a valid methodology to calculate non-financial benefits that were otherwise not adequately valued in the activities of job inclusion. This model is based on financial return on investment (ROI), a tool that is quite straightforward and commonplace within organizations. The ROI is the number of times an investment is earned back by the investor. However, because it is a financial measure, it fails to incorporate other returns that have been created for different stakeholders, such as social impacts. The SROI is designed to ascertain these values by expressing social value in monetary terms through a process known as monetization. It has to be noted that monetizing value is only a way to make it generally understandable and comparable. The SROI does not evaluate money; rather, it evaluates value creation using money as unit of measure. The principle is that because investments in social enterprises are monetary, the social value should be monetized as well, which makes it possible to state the size of the impact relative to investments (Olsen and Nicholls 2005).

This model has its roots in economic models such as cost-benefit and cost-effectiveness analysis, implemented to gauge the economic impact of social programs, most often as a policy tool used to influence levels of government spending (Levin 1983). Cost-benefit analysis can be carried out both in advance to determine whether an investment is likely to generate benefits superior to the next best alternative, and retrospectively to understand whether the investment was worthwhile. However, SROI differs from cost-benefit analysis in two ways. First, SROI is a practical management tool that enables informed decision-making on a regular basis, while social cost-benefit analysis is not used in regular business decision-making; rather, it is used periodically to determine the least expensive way to provide benefits or to reduce negative impacts to stakeholders. Second, SROI enables managers to maximize both social and financial benefits. In contrast, cost-benefit analysis typically frames benefits and costs as trade-offs and does not facilitate planning or prioritizing that optimizes both financial and social value creation (Lingane and Olsen 2004).

What this model proposes is a methodology of analysis and a formula to calculate the final value. The methodology is based on several leading principles:

- Involve stakeholders to understand their expectations, perceptions and needs and be sure that the provided information on impact evaluation is actually relevant for them.
- Measure both the positive and negative effects that can arise from a certain intervention.
- Measure both internal and external impacts such as corporate culture, employee satisfaction or environmental waste, and according to them identify an order of priorities on how to proceed both in the short and long term.
- Include only those impacts that can be realistically attributed to the organization/project, as several actors and external conditions can have a role in determining the pursued change.
- Do not overstate impacts, and do not include the same indicator in both the social and financial evaluations.
- Describe what makes a project better than existing ones, basing the evaluation process on a comparison between the social performance and the next best alternative, focusing not merely on the created benefit for society but also on the increased social impact compared to the activities of others.
- Quantify and monetize impact where possible, as not all the impacts can be accurately and significantly monetized, and misusing monetization can lead to wrong and too-subjective information.
- Consider the risk factors that could hamper the implementation of the model.
- Monitor results regularly, to understand any discrepancy and evaluate any improvement.

Stage 1	Stage 2		Stage 3		
Stakeholder	Input	Output	Outcome	Indicator	Financial proxy
Who do we have an effect on? Who has an effect on us?	What do they invest?	Summary of activities in numbers.	How can the change be described?	How can the change be measured?	What proxy can be used to value the change?

Stage 4				Stage 5				
Dead-weight (%)	Attribu-tion (%)	Drop Off (%)	Impact	Calculating SROI				
What would have happened without the activity?	Who else contributed to the change?	Does the outcome drop off in future years?	Quantity times financial proxy, less deadweight displace-ment and attribution	Year 1	Year 2	Year 3	Year 4	Year 5

Fig. 4.3 The Impact Map of SROI

The SROI approach is structured into three main steps:

(a) calculating the full blended value (economic and social value from a monetized perspective);
(b) calculating the total amount of financial investment;
(c) calculating the ratio between the full blended value (net of costs) and the financial investment, to generate a rate of return.

The hardest part is of course the first one, as it requires the identification and monetization of the generated social value. To this end, an impact map is drafted on the basis of the outcome pathway to: collect information about stakeholders, inputs, outputs, and outcomes; define indicators and financial proxies to value them (e.g. cost savings for the beneficiaries of a certain service or for public bodies, or the increasing of state revenues due to the taxes paid by new people entering the job market), as well as benchmark indicators based on how the change can be evaluated; establish the effective role of the organization in achieving the change; and calculate the monetized impact for a time horizon of five years.[2]

Figure 4.3 outlines the impact map for the SROI calculation.

[2] A five-year timeframe is the standard time horizon for SROI.

Box 4.1: Example of SROI calculation

Boyd (2004) proposes an interesting example to illustrate how SROI is implemented practically by social enterprises such as Tomorrow's People and its Get Out To Work (GOTW) program. The purpose of this program is to help people get a job in an area (Merseyside, UK) where employment, especially for young people with criminal records, can be difficult to find. The program's implementation costs £51,000 per year and its impact is evaluated against three main objectives: (1) help 163 offenders over the first 2 years; (2) ensure that at least 12 people find a job after the program; (3) reduce the reoffending rate. At the end of the first year GOTW was able to help 110 people, 19 of them were still employed after 10 months, and the reoffending rate was 15 % lower than the national average. The GOTW impact map is shown in Table 4.2. Using secondary data, the organization was able to estimate the percentage of people who would have found work without their help, and the social impact of GOTW was then calculated considering 17 long-term employees instead of 19.

Table 4.2 GOTW's impact map

Input	Output	Outcome	Impact
£51,000	110 people involved in the program	19 people find long-term employment	17 people with long term employment (deadweight accounted for)

Indirect 15 % reduction in reoffending

This outcome was then monetized using three different financial proxies: the benefit for the clients, coming from their income; the benefit for the state, coming from the reduction of money that it usually gives to the unemployed; and the reduction in reoffending, leading to lower crime-related costs. Using these financial proxies, the outcome was then monetized and projected onto a five-year timeframe, resulting in an overall social impact equal to £543,000. The SROI ratio is calculated as the ratio between the overall social impact and the required investment; for GOTW the result is equal to £543.000/ £51,000 = £10.5. This result expresses the amount of social impact that is created for every £1 spent on the program. For GOTW it is thus possible to say that for each £1 invested, the program is able to create £10.5 for society.

4.3.3 Social Balanced Scorecard

The social version of the Balanced Scorecard is another widely investigated and applied model, especially in relation to social enterprises (Emerson 2003; Rockefeller Foundation 2003; Lingane and Olsen 2004; Nicholls 2007; Boyer et al. 2008; Rinaldo 2010; Maas and Liket 2011). The Balanced Scorecard (BSC) is a strategic performance measurement and management tool (Kaplan and Norton 1996) designed for the private sector to support organizations in communicating their current state of operation and the path of development they aim to follow. It helps organizations to define their plans for translating their vision and strategies into concrete actions, and in so doing it provides four areas of analysis: (a) financial perspective—*how do we look to shareholders?*, (b) customer perspective—*how do customer see us?*, (c) business processes—*what must we excel at?*, and (d) learning and growth—*can we continue to improve and create value?* The inspiring principle is that organizations should not focus their attention only on financial outputs; instead, their main focus should be on what actually influences those financial outputs (e.g. process performance, market share, long-term learning, and skills development). Also, financial outputs are not always directly manageable by organizations, so it is better for them to include in their evaluation information on those areas where a direct management intervention is possible (Meadows and Pike 2010).

The four areas of analysis are connected to each other and, most of all, to the vision and the strategy of the organization. The first function of the BSC is to measure whether the smaller-scale operational activities of companies are actually aligned with their vision and strategy. Thus the focus is not only on financial outcomes; the operational, marketing and developmental inputs are also included in the analysis. This enables the BSC to provide a more comprehensive view of a business and drives companies to act according their long-term interests (Meadows and Pike 2010).

The BSC has been widely adopted as a tool for measuring external and internal economic value; however, the model does not include an employee, supplier or community perspective on an organization's performance (Mooraj et al. 1999), or considerations about the non-economic impact of activities on society and the environment. Starting from these limits and from the parallel urge for third-sector managers to measure and manage organizational performance, Kaplan (2001) worked on the adaptation of the BSC for non-profit organizations.

The need for change arises from the consideration that the initial focus in the application of the BSC for for-profit companies is the financial perspective, which provides a clear long-term objective for them, but is a constraint rather than an objective for non-profit organizations. Even if these organizations must monitor their spending and comply with financial budgets, their success cannot be measured only by financial information. What is then suggested by the author is to place the mission at the top of the scorecard, as it best reflects the organization's long-term objective. Also, there is a need for expanding the definition of who the customers are; as in non-profit organizations, those who pay and those who receive the benefits are different groups of stakeholders. Given these considerations, the BSC takes on a new configuration that best suits the needs of non-profit organizations.

As shown in Fig. 4.4, the traditional and social versions of the BSC differ in the weight of the elements that define the scheme of analysis. In the SBSC, the starting point is the pursued mission, which is directly connected to the two main categories of stakeholders: the donors and the customers. The choice of the business processes

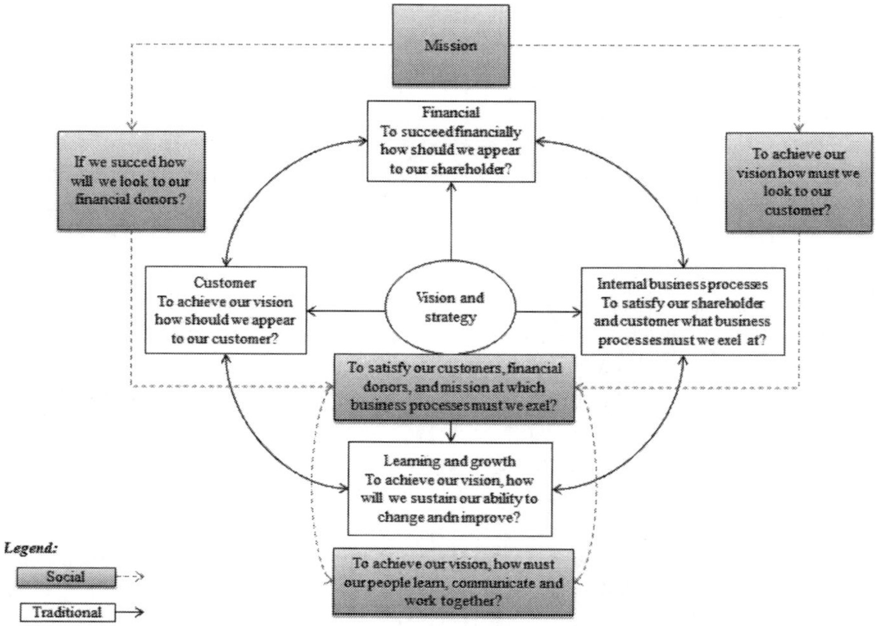

Fig. 4.4 From traditional to social BSC, adapted by Kaplan (2001)

and the practice of learning and growth are subordinated to the stakeholders' satisfaction, which goes together with the fulfilment of the mission.

The SBSC has been widely adopted by social enterprises, which often adapt the areas of inquiry or the methodology. Meadows and Pike (2010) partially modified the four categories, replacing them with: (a) business model; (b) financial return; (c) organizational development; and (d) social return on investment. This analysis is supposed to be applied three times in a timeframe of 10 years in order to assess the situation in the short, medium and long term, and avoid the criticisms aimed at the BSC about unclear temporal links between the analysed variables. Gomes and Liddle (2009) proposed a way of implementation that is slightly different, as it foresees the development of a SBSC for each business unit, rather than a unique framework for the whole organization.

Box 4.2: Example of Social Balanced Scorecard

In developing a social version of the traditional BSC, Kaplan (2001) analysed some examples of how this model could be applied by social enterprises. One of the case studies involves the Duke Children's Hospital (DCH). The initial situation of this organization was quite serious: it was losing money, staff members were dissatisfied, and the improvement initiatives developed up to that time had been unsuccessful. The SBSC was then used to reorganize the organization's activities around its mission, and to identify which kinds of interventions were actually more suited to addressing the situation. This tool is indeed very useful for defining the current situation and any room for improvement, and orienting all activities towards the achievement of the mission. The development of the SBSC at the DCH started with univocally defining the mission (see Fig. 4.5): to provide patients, families, and primary care physicians with the best, most compassionate care possible, and to excel at communication. To this end, communication and care were identified as the main points of the strategy to be pursued. Then, the SBSC was developed to screen initiatives and consider only those that could have a strong enough impact on the achievement of the mission. The satisfaction scores of families and primary care physicians increased with the improved services and the communication activities developed by the DCH. The cost per case dropped by 25 % in three years, and the average length of a stay dropped from eight to six days. Revenue increased, leading to a positive margin of about $10 million. The use of a SBSC to focus and align activities towards the achievement of the mission turned out to be a successful strategy for the DCH, enabling it to improve patient and physician satisfaction and achieve financial and operational improvements over a period of three years.

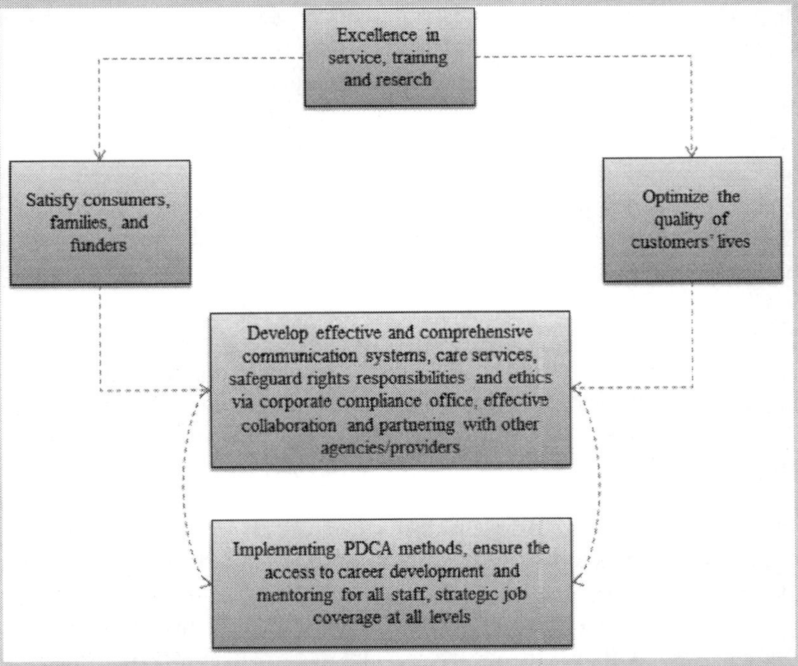

Fig. 4.5 The SBSC of the Duck's Children Hospital, adapted by Kaplan (2001)

4.4 The Rating Game: Monetizing Social Impact

What emerges from the outlined examples is that methods and frameworks share the same purpose but use methodologies and principles that are completely different. The focus of the methods must be the principle of monetization on which many of them are based, and which has been hotly debated in studies on SIA models. The growing interest in assessing social impact has its roots in the limitations of financial accounting, including the exclusion of non-monetized items, and of important categories of stakeholders such as employees, users or consumers of the service, society, government, volunteers, and members (Richmond et al. 2003). In the social sector financial ratios are no doubt important. The profit margin, for example, becomes a measure of surplus that can be used to support future activities rather than pay dividends to shareholders. But they fall far short of meeting the needs of mission-based performance, given that financial performance is often a means rather than an end to social sector activity (Ebrahim and Rangan 2010). Measuring social performance is a valuable activity, assuming that the ratings are consistently measured and accurately reflect the organization's social impact. Skepticism toward the possibility of accurately measuring qualitative data is among the main objections, as well as the high changeability of this kind of data that seriously restricts the possibility of finding common criteria. However, even when the criteria happen to be the same, they are invariably weighted differently in the final scoring (Porter and Kramer 2006). Therefore, the main risk is subjectivity in assessing social impacts, precisely because of the nature of the data to be measured. In this sense, monetizing social impact is intended as a way to have general, understandable, objective and comparable information about outcomes, as money is a language spoken by everybody.

The main limitation is the difficulty of finding financial proxies to monetize results. The European Venture Philanthropy Association (2008) collected information on existing ways to monetize social impacts. They found that two main options are available for the monetization of qualitative outcomes; the difference between them lies in the level of knowledge about costs and/or market prices for the selected indicators. This means that, for example, the reduction in job exclusion can be monetized as the saving on costs that would have been incurred for the state to support the unemployed participants. If either comparable costs or prices are known for the selected indicators, a set of techniques named cost price-based methods can be used; otherwise, value-based monetization methods can be used when no comparable data is known or available.

Cost price-based methods (or direct methods) are primarily used for infrastructure and large construction projects to analyse and highlight their total social costs and benefits. They underline not only the cost of construction, but also the cost of any restoration, repair or replacements; the cost of the loss of natural habitat; the effects on public health, and so on. In this sector these methods are widely known and used on a daily basis. They are mostly focused on highlighting the cost savings to show the minimum value created by the company. An interesting example is the *cost prevention method*, which consists of estimating the monetized value of a social outcome by estimating the cost price of those measures that prevent a further worsening of an undesirable situation; for example, the cost of buying healthy food to prevent employees from contracting diseases. A strong point of this method is that the values to which it refers are often simply market values. Another example is the *hedonic price method*, where the value of environmental factors is derived by the value difference that these factors create for an object in the environment. An example is the value difference between a house in a fashionable neighbourhood and the exact same house in a disadvantaged area. The increase in the value of the houses can be seen as indicator to determine the value of the increased feeling of security in the district.

However, methods like these can be limiting as they do not express other values that are less tangible but nevertheless important, such as the feeling of being involved again. Also, it is not always possible to find a comparable cost or price that can estimate the value of a social outcome. In this case, the value-based monetization method (also called the "contingent valuation method") consists of determining the value of a situation change by asking the stakeholders about it, focusing on their "willingness to pay" and/or "willingness to accept". A strong point of this method is that it asks the stakeholders directly about their perception of a change in their living environment. The weak point of this method, on the other hand, is that by asking people for their opinion, this method can be fairly subjective. There can always be a discrepancy between the expressed willingness to pay and the actual making of a payment (EVPA 2008).

4.5 The Need for Classification: A Proposed Taxonomy

The aim of giving an overview of existing models is to highlight an important issue concerning SIA, which is the confusion that can arise for managers when selecting from among the multitude of existing options. This wide range of models makes it hard for them to find out what methods are out there and which one could work for them. This is not an issue only for practitioners; it can also hamper the work of researchers involved in the development of new models, and academics when analysing the progress in SIA. An interesting but less expansive research field is addressing this issue by classifying the existing models and identifying common standards for their evaluation (Clark et al. 2004; Nicholls 2005; Olsen and Galimidi 2009a, b; Zappalà and Lyons 2009; Rinaldo 2010; Maas and Liket 2011). The main purpose of these studies is to define a set of criteria that allow organizations to better measure and communicate their social impact by following shared principles in selecting the most suitable model according to their needs.

Table 4.3 summarizes these classification systems.

These contributions present different examples of classifications. Some of these contain a less articulated structure, such as Nicholls' (2005), who classifies models according to the type of data required for the assessment (qualitative or quantitative), or Zappalà and Lyons' (2009), who focus on the model features to distinguish frameworks from methods. Others have proposed a more complex set of criteria with several variables, like Maas and Liket (2011), who selected six variables and 17 sub-variables of analysis. TRASI and NEF, instead, developed a sort of database where different models are presented according to their main features.

Grieco et al. (2014) started from the analysis of these classifications and developed an innovative taxonomy of SIA models. The gap they addressed was that in the existing classifications, models were analysed separately, and only their main features were illustrated. What was therefore missing was a classification system that organizes models according to different variables, creating macro-categories of models that are similar under different perspectives. None of the existing examples of classification identified groups of models that were internally homogenous yet heterogeneous with one another. This consideration was the starting point for the development of a taxonomy using variables drawn up from developed attempts.

The benefit of this approach is twofold: firstly, it helps social entrepreneurs to evaluate the complex array of existing models and choose the most suitable one for them, thus improving the practice of social impact assessment; and secondly, a comparison between models better shows their weakness and strengths. The identified macro-categories provide an overall frame of reference for understanding models and offer an overview which facilitates the identification and understanding of each model.

The variables they adopted for the taxonomy are as follows:

1. Data type: the nature of the data required for the assessment has a great influence on the model itself. In fact, qualitative data is usually more general and makes the overall model easier to apply; conversely, quantitative models require more specific information and data that may take more time to gather.
2. Impact type: as mentioned earlier, impact can refer to a variety of aspects. Holistic models tend to be general and assess the overall effect of the organizations' activities on surrounding areas. Other models are focused on specific kinds of impact that can affect: those working in the organizations (e.g. employee satisfaction, coherence with the social mission), the environment (e.g. waste production, noise pollution, sustainable development), the community (e.g. promoting further education, reducing poverty and social exclusion), or the economy (e.g. number of employees, increase in workforce).
3. Purpose: as organizations have different needs, they may have different reasons to implement SIA processes. Five of these were identified: screening (when the model is used to verify the achievement of specific goals), measuring (when it aims to accurately measure the impact generated), management (when the SIA process is carried out to assist managers in running their organization), certification (when the final aim is to obtain some external recognition for the organization), and reporting (when the objective is to account to stakeholders and a specific accounting structure is needed).
4. Model complexity: on the basis of number and type of indicators or categories provided for the study.
5. Sector: as models can be cross-sector or can be developed specifically for organizations working in a particular field, and this influences the indicators used and the information required.

Table 4.3 Attempts at classifications, adapted by Grieco et al. (2014)

Author(s)	Year	Variables (sub variables)
Clark et al.	2004	Functional category (process, impact, monetization)
		Impact value chain (input, activity, output, outcome, goal alignment)
		Lifecycle stage (start-up, expansion, maturity)
		Purpose (screening, partnership formation, management operation, scaling, external reporting, exit, retrospective evaluation)
		Cost/time
		Time breakdown (management, staff, third-party consultant, investor)
Nicholls	2005	Qualitative/quantitative
Zappalà and Lyons	2009	Methods/framework
Rinaldo	2010	Motivation (assessing effectiveness and/or efficiency, implementing change, quality mark, funder requirement)
		Readiness (defined/undefined social purpose)
		Capacity (small, medium, large)
		Impact type (environmental, economic, holistic, on volunteers)
Maas and Liket	2011	Purpose (screening, monitoring, reporting, evaluation)
		Timeframe (prospective, ongoing, retrospective)
		Orientation (input, output)
		Length of timeframe (short term, long term)
		Perspective (micro, meso, macro)
		Approach (process methods, impact methods, monetarization)
New Economics Foundation (NEF)		Organizational size (large, medium, small)
		Category of measure (strategy, quality, impact)
		Impact type (environmental, economic, holistic, people)
TRASI		Purpose (assessment, management, certification)
		Organization type (not-for-profit, government, foundation, social enterprise, social investor)
		Sector (general, specific)
		Focus (organizational effectiveness, social impact)
		Stage of the impact value chain (output, outcome, impact)

6. Timeframe: some models can be used prospectively to help managers decide whether the project should proceed as it is, proceed with certain changes, or be abandoned altogether. In other cases models are used as evaluative tools, to measure the achieved outcome against the intended objectives. Also, models can be structured to be applied as management tools, and be undertaken before, during and after the deployment of the organizations' projects.
7. Developer: many different actors are involved in the development of SIA models, and their diversity may be reflected in the models they produce.

Table 4.4 Overview of identified macro-categories of models, adapted by Grieco et al. (2014)

Macro-category	Data type	Impact type	Purpose	Model complexity	Sector	Time-frame	Developer
Simple social quantitative	Quant.	Society People	All	Simple	General	Retrosp.	All
Holistic complex	Quali-quant.	Holistic	Assessment reporting	Complex	General	Ongoing Retrosp.	Nonprofit network
Qualitative screening	Qual.	Holistic	All	Basic	Specific	Retrosp.	All
Management	Quali-quant.	All	Management certification	All	General	Ongoing	Consulting Firms Institutions

Analysing models according to these seven variables led the authors to identify four macro-categories of SIA models (see Table 4.4). This is an important output as it greatly simplifies the choice of the model to adopt, because looking at the features of each group, social entrepreneurs can make a first screening and focus directly on the group of models whose features can best meet the needs of their organizations.

In the following section each of the identified macro-categories of models will be presented as described by the authors, highlighting the variables that mostly characterize the whole group.

4.5.1 Simple Social Quantitative

The *simple social quantitative* (SSQ) group of models is characterized by by the type of required data and a low level of complexity. SSQ contains models based on quantitative indicators that are particularly focused on the assessment of social impact on communities and employees (e.g. increased lifespan of beneficiaries, employee satisfaction, organizational climate). For this reason these models are particularly suited for those social enterprises working in the fields of social care and assistance, or education and training, even if they are developed as applicable to all the sectors. The quantitative approach of the models enables them to precisely measure the generated impact, often in monetary terms. The timeframe of the analysis is retrospective; thus these models can be used to evaluate the results of implemented activities and are not particularly suited to estimating the outcomes in advance. These models are easy to apply, meaning that usually the whole model consists of no more than 15 indicators. The models in the SSQ group were proposed by a number of different promoters: research centres, universities, non-profit networks, non-profit organizations, and consulting firms and institutions.

Box 4.3: An example of SSQ models: Cost per Impact
Cost per Impact is a SIA model developed by the Center for High Impact Philanthropy (University of Pennsylvania), a non-profit and university-based

centre focused on improving the social impact of philanthropic activities. Their evaluative activity is based on identifying the link between costs and impact, to provide donors with information about where they can do the most good with the money they can invest. The approach is retrospective, as the model is based on information collected on the results of previous projects; however it has also an estimating value, as the output of the model allows future decisions to be focused on where to invest.

To provide a realistic estimate, this model combines the estimated costs with the empirical results from past implementations, providing information on the ratio between the incurred costs and the achieved outcomes. This calculation is created in three steps:

- Costs: in the best cases this includes both costs occurred in the past and the budget for future implementation. Only direct costs are included, and only the actual costs for philanthropists (excluding those costs covered by other partners). As total cost is not always easy to assess, it is often replaced with data on the cost per beneficiary.
- Results: obtained by past implementation. In keeping with the simplicity of the model, results only refer to the primary impact that the project produces, even if successful projects have multiple levels of additional benefits which, however, are more difficult to quantify or compare.
- Ratio: the costs are divided by the results to obtain a cost per (primary) impact evaluation.

Figure 4.6 shows which indicators were included to calculate the cost per impact of an educational program. The number of students enrolled in the program was divided by the number of those who showed improvement after participation, obtaining information about the success rate of the program. The result was then multiplied by the cost per beneficiary, estimating a cost-per-impact ratio.

Cost per beneficiary:	Success rate:	Cost per impact:
Cost of delivering program	Nr. of students in the program	Cost
Nr. of students in the program	Nr. of student changed by the program	Impact

Fig. 4.6 Cost per Impact analysis

4.5.2 Holistic Complex

The *holistic complex* (HC) models have as main features their wide approach to the generated impact, and a high level of complexity. This group contains models characterized by both qualitative and quantitative variables, ensuring a global view of outcomes that includes impact on communities, the environment, and the economy (a holistic approach, based on the overall added value). The combination of these data types results in the high degree of complexity of these models, that in some cases contain more than 100 indicators. The HC models are particularly focused on the reporting of results for reasons of stakeholder accountability. This means that in most cases they foresee the use of communication tools or ad hoc templates to facilitate the disclosure of the achieved results. This focus on reporting and communication makes HC models particularly suited for the purpose of obtaining funding. Models in the HC group can be applied to any sector, and have a timeframe that is ongoing or retrospective. They are developed primarily by non-profit networks.

Box 4.4: Example of HC models: the Sustainability Reporting Framework of GRI

The Sustainability Reporting Framework (SRF) is a set of reporting guidance materials developed by the Global Reporting Initiative (GRI). The GRI is an international non-profit organization active in the sustainability field. The support of sustainable activities is driven by the need for organizations to implement reporting activities in order to become more sustainable and make a better contribution to sustainable development. A core element in its activities is the SRF, which is widely used around the world. The purpose of this framework is to support organizations' reporting activities that disclose data about the economic, environmental and social impacts caused by their everyday activities. Through this model, the GRI aims to achieve its mission of making sustainability reporting standard practice for all kind of organizations, both for-profit and non-profit. Thus the SRF provides metrics and methods for measuring and reporting those impacts that are related to sustainable development. The framework includes a set of guidelines to drive the development of reports, as well as sector guidance to help practitioners adapt the model to their specific sector of activities. This model is quite complex due to its wide and holistic approach; it contains many indicators, both qualitative and quantitative. Its contents are summarized in the table below, which includes the categories of indicators divided into general and specific standard disclosures. By listing the standard disclosures an organization should make, the SRF clarifies the aspects on which an organization should focus when assessing the generated impact. Figure 4.7 lists the indicators identified in the SRF model.

General standard disclosure	Specific standard disclosure	
Report profile	Disclosures on management approach	
Organizational profile	Indicators:	
Identified material aspects and boundaries	**Economic** - economic performance - market presence - indirect economic impacts - procurement practice	**Environmental** - materials - energy - water - biodiversity - emissions - effluents and waste - products and services - compliance - transport - overall - supplier environmental assessment - environmental grievance mechanisms
Stakeholder engagement Strategy and analysis Governance Ethics and integrity	**Social** *Labor practices and decent work* - employment - labor/management relations - occupational health and safety - training and education - diversity and equal opportunity - equal remuneration for women and men - supplier assessment for labor practices - labor practices grievance mechanisms *Society* - local communities - anti-corruption - public policy - anti-competitive behavior - compliance - supplier assessment for impacts on society - grievance mechanisms for impacts on society	*Human rights* - Investment - Non-discrimination - Freedom of Association and Collective Bargaining - Child Labor - Forced or Compulsory Labor - Security Practices - Indigenous Rights - Assessment - Supplier Human Rights Assessment - Human Rights Grievance Mechanisms *Product responsibility* - Customer Health and Safety - Product and Service Labeling - Marketing Communications - Customer Privacy - Compliance

Fig. 4.7 General and specific standard indicators of the SRF

4.5.3 Qualitative Screening

The *qualitative screening* (QS) group of models is the largest one; it includes a wide range of framework and analysis schemes that are not based on the quantification or monetization of social outcomes. The nature of the required data is qualitative, which implies a low level of complexity because of the type and number of areas involved. Due to the nature of the data involved and the low level of complexity required, these models mostly perform screening purposes: instead of providing the organization with a specific measure of the generated social impact, they produce an overall view of the developed activities to assess whether or not the set objectives have been achieved, and if so, how. The QS models have a holistic approach, focusing on the whole value added by the assessed project, and the adopted timeframe is retrospective. They were developed by a variety of organizations (universities, research centres, non-profit networks, consulting firms), and they are the only group in which models for specific sectors are included (e.g. education, social care).

Box 4.5: Example of QS models: the Charity Analysis Framework

The Charity Analysis Framework (CAF) is a model produced by the New Philanthropic Capital (NPC) that provides selected qualitative indicators to help organizations identify whether they are tackling the most critical issues and making a significant difference to the life of the community, and whether they have the necessary ambition, leadership and resources they need to function properly. The NPC is a consulting organization that helps charities and funders successfully achieve their missions by developing an important research activity to identify new ways of working and prove the worthiness of their commitment. The CAF is a model based on the principle that periodic analysis can greatly benefit the activities of organizations and funders by helping them to identify the strengths and weaknesses in what they do, and improve their performances. However, it has been proved that this kind of analysis is underused both by charities and funders; nor do they understand how to approach it. CAF aims to assess the effectiveness of a charity's work, focusing on its ability to generate social impact, improve people's lives and create lasting change for the better.

Area of analysis	Assessment criteria		Grades
Activities	• Focus on greatest needs • Range of activities	• Ability to adapt and innovate • Links between activities	• Excellent • Good • Satisfactory • Below expectations
Results	• Results culture • Evidence of positive results	• Quality of evidence • Sharing results	
Leadership	• Management team • Governance	• Vision and strategy • Priorities	
People and resources	• Staff • Use of volunteers	• Other resources (such as IT, property and brand) • External leverage	
Finances	• Financial security • Quality of financial management	• Efficiency • Unit costs	
Ambition	• Potential to grow or replicate • Potential to improve results	• Potential to solve problems more widely • Willingness to change	

Fig. 4.8 Areas of analysis and assessment criteria of the CAF model

As shown in Fig. 4.8, the framework consists of six areas of analysis: activities, results, leadership, people and resources, finances, and ambition. For each of these, several indicators are provided to drive the assessment process. The indicators are evaluated using a grading grid that determines the level of performance for each, ranging from "excellent" to "below expectations". In this way organizations can gather evidence for how they are performing and identify any areas of improvement towards the achievement of their mission.

4.5.4 Management

The main feature of the *management* (MG) group of models is its purpose of managing the achievement of social impact through the whole development of the project. For this reason they have an ongoing approach aimed at including SIA as a lifelong process in the activities of the organization. The nature of the required data is both qualitative and quantitative, and the approach is holistic, ensuring a global view of the generated social impact. An important feature of MG models is that many of them foresee the obtainment of an external certification of the commitment, given by third parties, that confirms the system of impact management that the organization is putting in place. These models can be applied to every sector, and have been developed mostly by consulting firms and institutions.

Box 4.6: Example of MG: EMAS
The Eco Management and Audit Scheme (EMAS) is an environmental tool developed by the European Commission in order to help organizations evaluate and improve their environmental impact. The aim of this tool is twofold: it improves organizations' environmental performance, and supports communications to stakeholders and society in general about the organization's environmental achievements. EMAS was developed by the Environment Directorate General of the European Commission, set up in 1973 to ensure environmental protection. It therefore supports a proactive approach to environmental challenges and the search for innovative solutions to improve organizations' performances. This model has two main foci. First, its ongoing approach consists of establishing a system to monitor and manage the environmental impact of an organization's activities. In this way, environmental performance is continually assessed to ensure prompt action in case of misalignment from the set objective. Second, importance is given to the external certification of the organization's commitment, based on the transparency and credibility of its collected and disclosed information. Organizations that want to adopt the model are periodically evaluated by third-party entities that assess the compliance between statements and practice. When all the foreseen stages (see Fig. 4.9) of the model are developed and certified, organizations can use the EMAS logo as a public symbol of their voluntary adherence to the principles of environmental protection.

Stage	Description
1. Environmental review	Considering all environmental aspects of the organisation's activities, products and services, methods to assess these, relevant legal and regulatory framework and existing environmental management practices and procedures.
2. Environmental policy	Containing commitment both to comply with all relevant environmental legislation and to achieve continuous improvements in environmental performance.
3. Environmental programme	Information on specific environmental objectives and targets, to help the organisation in its everyday work when planning and implementing the improvements.
4. Environmental management system (EMS)	Aimed at achieving the organisation's environmental policy and at improving the environmental performance continually. The management system needs to set responsibilities, means to achieve objectives, operational procedures, training needs, monitoring and communication systems.
5. Environmental audit	Assessing in particular the management system in place and conformity with the organisation's policy and programme as well as compliance with relevant environmental regulatory requirements.
6. Environmental statement	Which lays down the results achieved against the environmental objectives and the future steps to be undertaken in order to continuously improve the organisation's environmental performance.
7. EMAS logo	All these stages must be approved by an accredited environmental verifier. The validated statement needs to be sent to the EMAS Competent Body for registration and made publicly available before an organisation can use the EMAS logo.

Fig. 4.9 The phases of the EMAS models

4.6 Does One Size Really Fit All? How to Choose the Model

Exploring the wide range of existing models allows an organization to underline their pros and cons as a whole. The multitude from which to choose can indeed be a strength of the implementation of SIA, as several tools are provided to those who want to implement this process. It can also, however, became a weakness, as there may simply be too many models, and they are often not generally known or understood (Grieco 2014). This can be an obstacle to the implementation of SIA, as social entrepreneurs may struggle to choose the best model for their organization from such a wide variety.

A key way to enhance the SIA process is to validate the wide landscape of models, highlighting the opportunity for social enterprises to find the one that best suits their needs, and this could be the solution to one of the bigger problems concerning models. The specificities of social enterprises cannot be translated into a "one-size-fits-all" model; yet the development of a specific approach tailored to each unique situation is unthinkable and is directly related to barriers such as a lack of benchmarks and resources, making it impossible to compare SIA results.

What is then needed are instruments that can drive the choices of social entrepreneurs, filling the gap of knowledge about the variety of models and the different needs they could meet. This consideration is the starting point for the development of an self-assessment of model categories that could connect social entrepreneurs and SIA models, supporting them in understanding their own needs concerning the assessment process, and in figuring out which main features the process must have; then proposing a set of models that actually fit the cases. Models range from very simple to highly complicated, though they can also be used as hints for the selection of indicators or processes to undertake.

The self-assessment starts from a set of considerations about the baseline situation that entrepreneurs must clarify:

- Which kind of impact do I want to assess? Do I want to have an overall vision of the effects that my activities have on the surrounding area? Do I want to focus on some specific aspect such as the impact on those who work in my organization, the community in which I operate, the natural environment, the creation of economic value for society?
- For what purpose am I implementing a SIA process? What kind of information do my stakeholders expect from me? Do I need to assess performances against set objectives, or a quantitative measure of what I'm doing for society, or an external certification? To which members of the public do I need to disclose this information?
- Which level of complexity can I deal with according to the money, time, skills, expertise and people I can dedicate to the implementation of the process?
- What timeframe do I need or want to adopt? Can SIA be more useful as a predictive tool, helping me to understand the possible outcome of a project under evaluation? Do I want to set a steady system of evaluations to assess and manage social impacts as they occur? Do I need to do an ex-post evaluation, gauging if the set objectives have been achieved through the implemented activities?
- What kind of data can I include in the SIA process, consistently with the purpose it has for my organization? Could numerical results be more adequate, or should I focus more on qualitative indicators? Could a mix of quantitative and qualitative data give a more complete view of what my organization is achieving through its operations?

This first analysis aims to gather evidence of the needs and the availabilities of the organization, so that the right model can be identified. The analysis of needs concerns the first two points: the type of impact on which to focus, and the kind of information that must be produced. These elements largely depend on stakeholders' requirements, whether they are funders who want information about the expected results of a project in which they are asked to invest, or volunteers and employees who need to be motivated by the social mission they are striving to achieve, or customers when competing in the market. The last three points refer to the analysis of the availabilities, and allow also an understanding of the number of resources that can be allocated to the development of a SIA process. Availabilities mainly concern decisions about

Which kind of impact do I want to assess?			
Holistic	Societal	Environmental	Economic
A-B-C	B-D	B	B-D

For which purpose?			
Screening	Reporting	Certification	Management
A-C-D	A-C-D	A-B-D	A-B-D

Which level of complexity can I deal with?		
Basic	Simple	Complex
A-B	B-D	B-C

Which timeframe to adopt?		
Perspective	Ongoing	Retrospective
A-B-C-D	B-C	A-C-D

Which kind of data to include?		
Qualitative	Quantitative	Quali-quantitative
A	D	B-C

Fig. 4.10 Self-assessment of model categories

data. This step of the analysis can be a starting point for the entrepreneur in deciding whether to focus on the data at his or her disposal, or if an investment in further research for new data collection could be worthwhile. The analysis of the foci of availabilities is essential in order to make decisions about the timeframe of the analysis (as using data on past implementation can be easier than the estimation of results in advance), the level of complexity of the overall process (the easier the model is to use, the fewer resources are needed), and the type of data to include (qualitative, quantitative or both, according to what is available and the purpose).

Clarifying these elements allows an entrepreneur to define an initial idea of how the approach to the assessment process could be undertaken. The decisions on these points are also the basis of the self-assessment, which drives entrepreneurs to use a set of models that can meet the emerging needs. In Fig. 4.10, each question is directly linked to one of the groups of models outlined above. This means that according to the configuration of the single variables included in the self-assessment, a group of models may emerge as the best option to choose from which to find a model that best fits with the expressed needs and availabilities of the organization.

Table 4.5 Prevailing answers and related models

Prevailing answer	Group	Included models (for a more detailed view of these models, please see Annex A.)
A	Qualitative screening (QS)	Atkisson compass assessment for investors
		BoP impact assessment framework
		Cooperatives performance indicators—CESPI
		Fit for purpose
		European foundation for quality management
		Logic model builder
		Prove it!
		Social IMPact measurement for local economies (SIMPLE)
		Volunteering impact assessment toolkit
		The values based checklist for social firms
		Assessment and improvement indicators
		Charity analysis framework
		Echoing green mid-year and year end report
		Progress out of poverty index (PPI)
		SCALERS
		Wallace assessment tool
		TBL scorecard
		Ongoing assessment of social impacts—OASIS
		Public value scorecard
		Social compatibility analysis
		Social return assessment
		Wellventure monitor
		Social enterprise mark
		Wellbeing measure
		Family of measures
		SIM tool survey
B	Management (MG)	Eco-mapping
		EMAS
		Investors in people
		Quality first
		The big picture
		Cradle to cradle certification
		Trucost
		The B impact rating system
		Toolbox for analyzing sustainable ventures in developing countries
		Socio-economic assessment toolbox
		Community impact mapping
		Outcome star
		C3 perform
		Customer service excellence

(continued)

Table 4.5 (continued)

Prevailing answer	Group	Included models (for a more detailed view of these models, please see Annex A.)
C	Holistic complex (HC)	AA1000
		GRI sustainability reporting framework
		Measuring impact framework
		Millennium development goal scan
		Practical quality assurance system for small organizations
		SOCIAL
		Social investment risk assessment
		Social accounting and audit
		Third sector performance dashboard
		Impact reporting and investment standard
		GIIRS
		Social enterprise balanced scorecard
		HIP (human impact + profit) scorecard
		Methodology for impact analysis and assessment
		Success measures data system
		Acumen scorecard
		Charity assessment method of performance
		Participatory impact assessment
		Star social firm
		COSA methodology
D	Simple social Quantitative (SSQ)	SOUL (soft outcomes universal learning) Record
		Best available charitable option (BACO)
		Local multiplier 3
		Social return on investment—SROI
		MicroRate
		Movement above the U.S. $1 a day threshold
		Pulse—portfolio data management system
		Expected return
		The FINCA client assessment tool
		Social value metrics
		Social rating
		Social performance indicators
		Cost per impact
		Social footprint
		Stakeholder value added
		Business ethic excellence model

As shown in Table 4.5, the intended outcome of this self-assessment is a group of models that emerges as the preferred option, according to the specific requirements of the organization. Of course it has to be considered that models within the same group can be slightly different from each other, but indications for which group on which to focus allow a first screening of the whole landscape of models and support the implementers orienting the choosing process.

References

Antonaras, A., Iacovidou, M., & Memtsa, C. (2011). Measuring social return on investment using the EBEN GR Business Ethics Excellence Model. *Current Issues of Business and Law, 6*(1), 69–89.

Bloom, P., & Chatterji, A. K. (2009). Scaling social entrepreneurial impact. *California Management Review, 51*(3), 114–133.

Boyd, J. (2004). *Measuring social impact: The foundation of social return on investment (SROI)*. London Business School. http://sroi.london.edu/Measuring-Social-Impact.pdf. Accessed 15 May 2013.

Boyer, D., Creech, H., & Paas, L. (2008). *Critical success factors and performance measures for start-up social and environmental enterprises*. Report for SEED Initiative Research Programme, International Institution for Sustainable Development (IISD).

Clark, C., Rosenzweig, W., Long, D., & Olsen, S. (2004). Double bottom line project report: Assessing social impact in double bottom line ventures. http://www.riseproject.org/DBL_Methods_Catalog.pdf.

Council for social development. (2010). *Social impact assessment*, Report of a research project on social impact assessment of R&R policies and packages in India, New Delhi.

Ebrahim, A. S., & Rangan, V. K. (2010). *The limits of non-profit impact: A contingency framework for measuring social performance*. Harvard Business School General Management Unit Working Paper (10-099).

Emerson, J. (2003). The blended value preposition: Integrating social and financial return. *California Management Review, 45*(4), 35–51.

Epstein, M. J., & Yuthas K. (2014). *Measuring and improving social impacts: A Guide for non-profits, companies, and impact investors*. BK Business.

Esteves, A. M., & Vanclay, F. (2009). Social development needs analysis as a tool for SIA to guide corporate-community investment: Applications in the minerals industry. *Environmental Impact Assessment, 29*(2), 137–145.

EVPA. (2008). SROI methodology an introduction. http://evpa.eu.com/wp-content/uploads/2010/09/SOCIAL-EVALUATOR-SROI-an-introduction.pdf.

Gomes, R. C., & Liddle, J. (2009). The balanced scorecard as a performance management tool for third sector organizations: The case of the Arthur Bernardes Foundation, Brazil. http://www.anpad.org.br/bar.

Grieco, C. (2014). *Exploring Italian Social Enterprises Coherence in Social Impact Assessment, Conference Proceedings Euram Annual Conference, Valencia*. June 4–7, 2014.

Grieco, C., Michelini, L., & Iasevoli, G. (2014). Measuring value creation in social enterprises a cluster analysis of social impact assessment models. Nonprofit and voluntary sector quarterly, 0899764014555986.

Hart, T., & Haughton, G. (2007). *Assessing the economic and social impacts of social enterprise*. Centre for City and Regional Studies, University of Hull. https://www.escholar.manchester.ac.uk/. Accessed June 15, 2012.

Hehenberger, L., Harling, A. M., & Scholten P. (2013). *A practical guide to measuring and managing impact*. European Venture Philanthropy Association.

Interorganizational Committee on Guidelines and Principles for Social Impact Assessment. (1994). Guidelines and principles for social impact assessment. *Impact Assessment, 12*(2), 107–152.

Kaplan, R. S. (2001). Strategic performance measurement and management in non-profit organizations. *Non-profit Management and Leadership, 11*(3), 353–370.

Kaplan, R. S., & Norton, D. P. (1996). *The balanced scorecard: Translating strategy into action*. Boston: Harvard Business Press.

Levin, H. M. (1983). *Cost-effectiveness: A primer*. Beverly Hills: Sage.

Lingane, A., & Olsen, S. (2004). Guidelines for social return on investment. *California Management Review, 46*(3), 135–166.

Lockie, S. (2001). SIA in review: Setting the agenda for impact assessment in the 21st century. *Impact Assessment and Project Appraisal, 19*(4), 277–288.

Maas, K., Liket, K. (2011). Social impact measurement: Classification of methods. In R. Burritt, S. Schaltegger, M. Bennett, T. Pohjola, & M. Csutora (Eds.), *Environmental management accounting and supply chain management, eco-efficiency in industry and science* (Vol. 27, pp. 171–202).

Meadows, M., & Pike, M. (2010). Performance management for social enterprises. *Systemic Practice and Action Research, 23*(2), 127–141.

Mooraj, S., Oyon, D., & Hostettler, D. (1999). The balanced scorecard: A necessary good or an unnecessary evil? *European Management Journal, 17*(5), 481–491.

Nicholls, A. (2005). *Measuring impact in social entrepreneurship: New accountabilities to stakeholders and investors?*. Oxford, UK: Skoll Centre for Social Entrepreneurship, University of Oxford.

Nicholls, J. (2007). *Why measuring and communicating social value can help social enterprise become more competitive*. Cabine Office, Office of the Third Sector. http://evpa.eu.com/wp-content/uploads/2010/09/Why-measuring-and-communicating-social-value-can-help-social-enterprise-become-more-competitive1.pdf.

Olsen, S., & Galimidi, B. (2009a). Managing social and environmental impact: A new discipline for a new economy. *Brown Journal of World Affairs, 15*(2), 43–56.

Olsen, S., & Galimidi, B. (2009b). Managing social and environmental impact: A new discipline for a new economy. *Brown Journal of World Affairs, 15*(2), 43–56.

Olsen, S., & Nicholls, J. (2005). A framework for approaches to SROI analysis. http://ccednet-rcdec.ca/sites/ccednet-rcdec.ca/files/ccednet/pdfs/2005-050624_SROI_Framework.pdf. Accessed Nov, 2013.

Perrini, F., & Vurro, C. (2013). La valutazione degli impatti sociali, Egea.

Porter, M. E., & Kramer, M. R. (2006). Strategy and society. *Harvard Business Review, 84*(12), 78–92.

Richmond, B. J., Mook, L., & Quarter, J. (2003). Social accounting for non profits. Two models. *Non-profit Management & Leadership, 13*(4), 308–324.

Rinaldo, H. (2010). Getting started in social impact measurement. The Guild. http://www.gaugeni.co.uk/sites/default/files/Getting%20started%20in%20social%20impact%20measurement.pdf.

Rockefeller Foundation, The Goldman Sachs Foundation. (2003). Social impact assessment: A discussion among grant makers. Meeting proceedings, New York City.

Sawhill, J. C., & Williamson, D. (2001). Mission impossible? Measuring success in non-profit organizations. *Non-profit Management & Leadership, 11*(3), 371–386.

Vanclay, F. (2003). International principles for social impact assessment. *Impact Assessment and Project Appraisal, 21*(1), 5–11.

Zappalà, G. Lyons, M. (2009). Recent approaches to measuring social impact in the third sector: An overview. Centre for Social Impact, Background Paper, no. 5 http://www.csi.edu.au/assets/assetdoc/b20aada17ffad8f7/V2%20CSI%20Background%20Paper%20No%205%20%20Approaches%20to%20measuring%20social%20impact.pdf.

Annex A
Overview of Existing Models

Abstract In these Annex, 76 models of SIA are described. A brief table is proposed for each model, giving information about the promoter, the purpose of the model and its main contents, and a source for further information.

Qualitative Screening Models

Atkisson compass assessment for investors	
Developed by	Atkisson Inc.
Purpose	To measure an organization's impact referring to the analyzed variables
Content	The method incorporates a structure with five key areas: N = nature (environmental benefits and impacts) S = society (community impacts and involvement) E = economy (financial health and economic influence), and W = well-being (effect on individual quality of life), and a fifth element, + = Synergy (links between the other four areas and networking), and includes a point-scale rating system on each of the five areas. Each area has several indicators each of which has specific criteria. The method has been peer reviewed by corporate executives, economic academicians, and investment professionals
Source	http://www.atkisson.com/wwd_tools.php

BoP impact assessment framework	
Developed by	William Davidson Institute (Ted London)
Purpose	To assess the well-being an organization create for three categories of stakeholders: sellers, buyers and community
Content	It helps organizations better understand and improve their on-the-ground poverty alleviation impacts. The BoP Framework provides managers with a robust and systematic approach to conducting: (1) a strategic analysis to gain a deep understanding of their holistic set of impacts, and (2) a performance analysis to identify, track, and improve key indicators over time
Source	http://bop2009.org/ia.aspx#Tool

C. Grieco, *Assessing Social Impact of Social Enterprises*,
SpringerBriefs in Business, DOI 10.1007/978-3-319-15314-8

Cooperatives performance indicators—CESPI	
Developed by	Co-operatives commission UK
Purpose	To measure non-financial performance of co-operatives as environmental and social ones
Content	Ten principles: (1) member economic involvement; (2) member democratic partecipation; (3) partecipation of empoloyees and members in training and education; (4) staff injury and absentee rates; (5) staff profile—gender and ethnicity; (6) customer satisfaction; (7) consideration of ethical issues in procurement and investmen decisione; (8) investment in community and co-operative initiatives; (9) net carbon dioxide emissions arising from operations; (10) proportion of waste recycled/reused
Source	http://www.uk.coop/cespis

Fit for purpose	
Developed by	Development trusts association
Purpose	To help community organizations assessing strengths and areas of improvements in their efforts toward the social mission
Content	Seven indicators for each of the following areas: (1) Governance; (2) Enterprise and business planning; (3) Financial management; (4) Partnership working; (5) Policies and procedures
Source	http://locality.org.uk/resources/fit-purpose-healthcheck-community-organisations/

European foundation for quality management	
Developed by	British quality foundation (BQF)
Purpose	To help community organizations assessing strengths and areas of improvements in their efforts toward the social mission
Content	There are nine criteria separated into Enablers and Results. The Enablers are concerned with how an organization conducts itself, how it manages its staff and resources, how it plans its strategy and how it reviews and monitors key processes (1) Leadership; (2) People; (3) Policy and strategy; (4) Partnership and resources; (5) Processes. The results are what it achieves (6) People results; (7) Costumer results; (8) Society results; (9) key performance results. Each of them is subdivided to describe in more detail the concept of Excellence in each area
Source	http://www.bqf.org.uk/efqm-excellence-model

Logic model builder	
Developed by	Innovation network
Purpose	To provide organizations with a framework that shows how inputs and output are linked to outcomes
Content	Resources/Input → Activities → Output → Outcomes → Impact
Source	http://toolkit.childwelfare.gov/toolkit/assets/pdfs/logicmodel.pdf;jsessionid=02302e9f4e80844ab3a4246e3033e33183da

Prove it!	
Developed by	New economic foundation (NEF)
Purpose	To assess the influence of community regeneration projects on local people quality of life
Content	This tool provides a method for measuring the effect of community regeneration projects on the quality of life of local people
Source	http://www.proveit.org.uk/

Social IMPact Measurement for Local Economies (SIMPLE)	
Developed by	Social Enterprise London (SEL) and University of Brighton
Purpose	To assess organizations' impact on community
Content	It's a framework representing a five-stage approach that an organization can undertake to identify, measure and communicate its impact: (1) Scope it; (2) Map it; (3) Track it; (4) Tell it; (5) Embed it
Source	http://www.sel.org.uk/impact-assessment.aspx

Volunteering impact assessment toolkit	
Developed by	Institute for volunteering research
Purpose	To help organizations in measure and assess the impact of volunteering
Content	It's aimed to give organizations a clearer understanding of the impact of volunteering activity on the four main stakeholder groups involved: the volunteers; the host organization; the service users and the wider community. The Volunteering Impact Assessment Toolkit itself consists of a set of ready-made core questionnaires and supplementary questionnaires designed for use with people from each of the four stakeholder groups. Each core questionnaire has a small number of questions for each topic or 'capital' area
Source	http://www.ivr.org.uk/component/ivr/volunteering-impact-assessment-toolkit-a-practical-guide-for-measuring-volunteering&qh=YToyOntpOjA7czo3OiJ0b29sa2l0IjtpOjE7czo4OiJ0b29sa2l0cyI7fQ==

The values based checklist for social firms	
Developed by	Social firms UK
Purpose	To bring recognition to Social Firms that meet all of the essential values, enabling them to effectively communicate their status within the sector
Content	This checklist is designed to bring clarity in understanding Social Firms and is structured on the three core values of the sector: enterprise, employment and empowerment
Source	http://www.socialfirmsuk.co.uk/resources/library/values-based-checklist

Assessment and improvement indicators	
Developed by	Venture Philantropy Partners
Purpose	To convey the quality of performance an organization has in 13 specific organizational categories and how much it has improved and changed in each area
Content	This assessment tool uses two sets of indicators, one to show how much an organization has improved and changed in each area and another to represent the actual quality of performance in each area
Source	http://www.vppartners.org/results/how-we-assess

Charity analysis framework	
Developed by	New Philantropy Capital
Purpose	To evaluate grantees in the human welfare sector.
Content	Its analysis focuses on several criteria within six key areas: activities, results, leadership, staff and other resources, finances and ambition, in order to answer the following questions: (1) Is the charity tackling the most important issues?; (2) Is it tackling them in ways that make a significant difference?; (3) Has it got ambition, leadership and resources to continue to be effective? The results are also displayed in a Grading Grid, ranging from Excellent to Below Expectations
Source	http://www.philanthropycapital.org/publications/improving_the_sector/charity_analysis/little_blue_book.aspx

Echoing green mid-year and year end report	
Developed by	Echoing green
Purpose	To assess the ongoing impact of an organization receiving funds to do social sector work
Content	It uses a mid-year and year end survey to assess program development, organizational development, community outreach, program sustainability, personal and professional development, and outcome tracking and sustainability
Source	Kramer 2005 Measuring Innovation, Appendix B

Progress out of poverty index (PPI)	
Developed by	Grameen foundation
Purpose	To evaluate the number of microfinance clients that moves out of poverty over time
Content	The PPI asks 10 questions that are predictive of poverty
Source	http://www.progressoutofpoverty.org/understanding-the-progress-out-poverty-index

SCALERS	
Developed by	Bloom and Chatterji
Purpose	To help social enterprises scaling their impact
Content	The model introduces a conceptual model that proposes seven drivers—or organizational capabilities—that can stimulate successful scaling by asocial entrepreneurial organization. These drivers/capabilities are identified by using the acronym SCALERS, which stands for: Staffing, Communications, Alliance building, Lobbying, Earnings generation, Replication, and Stimulating market forces. The model also proposes that the extent to which an individual SCALERS (i.e., driver or capability)will influence scaling success will depend on certain situational contingencies
Source	California Management Review, Vol 51 No. 3, 2009

Wallace Assessment Tool	
Developed by	Wallace foundation
Purpose	This is a method to assess foundation impact
Content	The method asks four core questions with varying indicators by program area. The questions are: (1) Are our grantee partners satisfactorily executing their plans? (2) Are our partners incorporating the changes they are making in the way they do their work? (3) Are people in our grantee sites benefiting? (4) Are we producing and effectively promoting useful knowledge?
Source	http://www.wallacefoundation.org/knowledge-center/advancing-philanthropy/Documents/How-Are-We-Doing-Foundations-Effort-to-Gauge-its-Effectiveness.pdf

TBL Scorecard	
Developed by	Triple bottom line collaborative
Purpose	To measure the so-called Triple Bottom Line deals (Equity, Environment and Economic)
Content	The requirement for this designation was that a TBL loan needed to have at least one metric or impact in each of the three categories of social returns: economy, equity, and environment
Source	http://trasi.foundationcenter.org/record.php?SN=135

Ongoing Assessment of Social Impacts—OASIS	
Developed by	REDF
Purpose	To assess the social outputs and outcomes of social enterprises
Content	It foresees 7 steps: (1) convene a working group; (2) identify key staff; (3) establish consulting partners; (4) assessment of organizational client-related information needs; (5) design of the client tracking system; (6) automation; (7) implementation and beyond
Source	http://redf.org/wordpress/wp-content/uploads/2013/10/REDF-An-Information-OASIS-Comprehensive-and-Customized-Client-Information-and-Tracking-Systems-Publication-2002.pdf

Public value scorecard	
Developed by	Prof. M.H. Moore, Director of the Hauser Center for Non-profit Corporations at the John F. Kennedy School of Government at Harvard University
Purpose	It is an adaptation of Balanced Scorecard, to meet the needs of non-profit organizations
Content	There are three crucial differences between the BSc and the PVSc. First, in the public value scorecard, the ultimate value to be produced by the organization is measured in non-financial terms. Second, the public value scorecard focuses attention not just on those customers who pay for the service, or the clients who benefit from the organization's operations; it focuses as well on the third party payers. Third, the public value scorecard focuses attention on productive capabilities for achieving large social results outside the boundary of the organization itself'
Source	http://www.exinfm.com/workshop_files/public_sector_scorecard.pdf

Social compatibility analysis	
Developed by	Institute for Sustainable Development
Purpose	It helps including social compatibility in planning processes
Content	The SCA defines objective criteria according to which social compatibility is evaluated for projects, products, organizations.
Source	http://www.bfs.admin.ch/bfs/portal/en/index/themen/21/11/visu/03.parsys.0012.downloadList.00121.DownloadFile.tmp/vonallmenposter.pdf

Social Return Assessment	
Developed by	Pacific community ventures
Purpose	Assessing the social return of each investor and of its portfolio overall.
Content	The system entails tracking progress specifically on the number and quality of jobs created by PCV's portfolio corporations. It helps the fund target and improve its services to its investors and to a group of corporations to which it provides business advisory services
Source	https://business.ualberta.ca/-/media/business/centres/cccsr/ccse/documents/generalinformation/papers/paperrosenzweig.pdf

Wellventure monitor	
Developed by	Fortis Foundation Netherlands (FFN) and Erasmus University Rotterdam (EUR)
Purpose	It measures the effects of community investment on several aspects. It makes clear what the target group benefits from the project, but also what the corporation, the employees, and the social organization gains from it
Content	The Wellventure Monitor™ provides insight into the effects of a specific project. But more importantly; it is also possible to see the sum of the different projects. This way, the long-term benefits of community investment become visible. With the tool, corporations and corporations can create a survey after finishing a project and send it to those involved at the corporation, employees of the organization, and to the target group. The surveys are processed automatically. The tool can be used to view, analyze, and present the results. Per project, or over a longer period of time'
Source	http://www.mvonederland.nl/mvo-tool/wellventure-monitor

(67) Social Enterprise Mark	
Developed by	Social enterprise mark company
Purpose	The Mark is awarded to businesses who meet specific criteria that demonstrate they are working primarily for social and/or environmental goals, and that 50 % of their profits are reinvested towards those goals
Content	Several criteria have to be meet: have social or environmental aims; have own constitution and governance; earn at least 50 % income from trading (new starts pledge to meet this within 18 months); spend at least 50 % profits fulfilling social or environmental aims; distribute residual assets to social or environmental aims, if dissolved; demonstrate social value
Source	http://www.socialenterprisemark.org.uk/

Wellbeing measure	
Developed by	New Philanthropy Capital
Purpose	It is an online survey-based tool designed to help charities, schools and other organizations show the difference they make to the lives of young people
Content	It covers eight aspects of the well-being of 11–16 year olds: Self-esteem; emotional wellbeing, resilience, satisfaction with friends, satisfaction with family, satisfaction with community, satisfaction with school, life satisfaction
Source	http://www.thinknpc.org/our-work/our-services/npcs-well-being-measure-2/

Family of measures	
Developed by	Sawhill and Williamson
Purpose	To help organizations in better articulate a venture's progress towards its mission objectives
Content	This models is built around three sets of linked metrics: impact measures, activity measures, capacity measures. It consists of a core structure of mission, goals and strategies, connected to three points of measurement: Impact, Capacity, and Activity. Impact measures the success at accomplishing their mission. Capacity measures their financial strength e.g. success of their fundraising and overall ability to support their business activities. Activity measures the success of achieving goals and implementing strategies
Source	Sawhill J., Williamson D. (2001), Measuring what matters in non-profit, McKinsey Quarterly

SIM tool survey	
Developed by	INAFI
Purpose	It is an internet-based tool to measure and report on social impact of their work of Microfinance intervention and their programs in terms of changes in the lives of clients and families
Content	The model contains ten criteria which are divided in three areas: standard corporate code, corporate governance and corporate social responsibility
Source	http://www.sim-inafi.org/

Management Models

Eco-mapping	
Developed by	Heinz-Werner Engel in "International Network for Environmental Management (INEM) e Eco Management and Audit Scheme (EMAS) Tool Kit per PMI" project
Purpose	To assess environmental impact of organizations
Content	Helps organizations in creating a map to understand their impact on environment and especially on: (1) Urban situation; (2) Nuisances; (3) Water; (4) Soil; (5) Air, odors, noise, dust; (6) Energy; (7) Waste; (8) Risks. Organizations have to map all these items to understand if they are small problems to be monitored or big issues to face with
Source	http://www.ecomapping.org/en/index.html

EMAS	
Developed by	European commission
Purpose	To help organization evaluate and improve their environmental impact
Content	There are 4 stages: (1) Conducting and environmental review; (2) Establish an environmental management system; (3) Carry out an internal environmental audit; (4) Provide a statement
Source	http://ec.europa.eu/environment/emas/index_en.htm

Investors in people	
Developed by	UK commission for employment and skills
Purpose	To assess and improve organizations' performance by managing and developing human resources (employees)
Content	It's addressed to employees to make organizations able to work on their performance towards people. It follows the process: Plan—Do—Review
Source	http://www.investorsinpeople.co.uk/Interactive/pages/LinksManagementpages.aspx

Quality first	
Developed by	Birmingham voluntary service council
Purpose	To help management running effectively and efficiently the organizations. It is aimed at small organizations that are run solely by volunteers, though may be used by organizations with one or two paid staff
Content	There are 9 area of quality each of them with 2 level of implementation
Source	www.bvsc.org http://www.proveandimprove.org/tools/qualityfirst.php#Section8

The Big Picture	
Developed by	Scottish council voluntary organizations
Purpose	To help management running effectively and efficiently the organizations
Content	It helps identifying the strengths and weaknesses of an organization across all its activities. It is non-prescriptive and does not involve strictly following a set of rules or standards, but provides a broad and coherent set of assumptions about what is required for a good organization and its management
Source	http://www.evaluationsupportscotland.org.uk/media/uploads/resources/introducingthebigpicture.pdf

Cradle to Cradle Certification	
Developed by	Cradle to Cradle Product Innovation Institute
Purpose	To assess the environmental impact of organizations and help them manage and improve it
Content	It offers a tool that certifies companies that meet a standard for using environmentally safe and healthy materials; design for material reutilization, such as recycling or composting; the use of renewable energy and energy efficiency; efficient use of water, and maximum water quality associated with production; and instituting strategies for social responsibility. If a candidate product achieves the necessary criteria, it is certified as a Basic, Silver, Gold or Platinum product and can be branded as Cradle to Cradle CertifiedCM
Source	http://www.c2ccertified.org/

Trucost	
Developed by	Trucost PLC
Purpose	To see and manage their environmental impact
Content	It rates the efficiency of a company's operations and provides clients with an understanding of the financial risks to a company if it had to pay for its environmental impacts. A global input-output model is used to estimate the amount of resources a company uses to produce goods or services and the related level of pollutants
Source	http://www.trucost.com/what-we-do

The B Impact Rating System	
Developed by	B Lab
Purpose	To measure a company's social and environmental impact
Content	It foresees three stages: (1) assess company's performance against best practices on employee, community, and environmental impact; (2) compare impact against other businesses; (3) create a plan to improve company's practices, and help the staff implement them easily with the Best Practice Guides and Examples
Source	http://bimpactassessment.net/

Toolbox for analyzing sustainable ventures in developing countries	
Developed by	UNEP
Purpose	The toolbox is developed to answer questions related to the identification of opportunities, the understanding of the determinants of success and the assessment of costs and benefits appear repeatedly
Content	The tools respond to three questions that appear over and again in the process of building and managing a sustainable venture: (1) Where are opportunities to create value • by meeting needs better and more efficiently? (2) What factors determine the success of the venture? (3) What are costs and benefits of the venture for the business, society and the environment?
Source	http://www.unep.fr/scp/publications/details.asp?id=DTI/1136/PA

Socio-economic assessment toolbox	
Developed by	Anglo American
Purpose	It is an effective process to help create and implement your sustainable development policies, to make sure a company's presence accords with your neighbors' own aspirations and best interests, you need an
Content	The SEAT process is divided into seven steps, with each step supported by a number of tools: (1) Profile the Anglo American operation and the host community; (2) Engage with stakeholders; (3) Assess and prioritise impacts and issues; (4) Improve social performance management—how we interact with our stakeholders; (5) Deliver enhanced socio-economic benefits to host communities; (6) Develop a social management plan; (7) Prepare a SEAT report and feedback to stakeholders
Source	http://www.angloamerican.com/development/social/seat/

(68) Community impact mapping	
Developed by	Development trust association
Purpose	It helps organizations start to think about their story, why and how they do what they do. It is a simple way to visualize their journey and the difference they are making to community
Content	It foresees the definition of a storyboard: Vision—what did you want to achieve for your community? What did you use—Staff? Volunteers? Money? Activities—what did you do with the resources? What happened because of what you did? What difference did your actions make to your community?
Source	http://portals.wi.wur.nl/files/docs/ppme/impactmapping.pdf

Outcome star	
Developed by	Triangle consulting social enterprise
Purpose	It is a suite of tools for supporting and measuring change when working with people
Content	All versions consists of a number of scales based on an explicit model of change which creates coherence across the whole tool and a Star Chart onto which the service user and worker plot where the service user is on their journey. The attitudes and behavior expected at each of the points on each scale are clearly defined, usually in detailed scale descriptions, summary ladders or a quiz format. Each step on the ladder is associated with a numerical score so at the end of the process the scores can be plotted onto the service user's Star. The process is then repeated at regular intervals (every three, six or 12 months depending on the project) to track progress
Source	http://www.outcomesstar.org.uk/

Customer service excellence	
Developed by	EMCQ
Purpose	It aims to make a tangible difference to service users by encouraging provider organizations to focus on their individual needs and preferences
Content	Five criteria have to be met to obtain the certification: customer insight, culture of organization, information and access, delivery, timeliness and quality of service
Source	http://www.customerserviceexcellence.uk.com/standardRequirementCSE.html

Holistic Complex Models

(AA1000)	
Developed by	Account ability
Purpose	To ensure the reliability of organizations' reports
Content	Principles of materiality, completeness, responsiveness. It focuses on measuring whether an organization achieves its desired social impact
Source	www.accountability.org

GRI sustainability reporting framework	
Developed by	Global reporting initiative
Purpose	To assess organizations' sustainability
Content	There are 4 key elements in the framework: (1) Sustainability reporting guidelines; (2) Indicator protocol; (3) Sector supplements; (4) Technical protocols
Source	https://www.globalreporting.org/reporting/reporting-framework-overview/Pages/default.aspx

Measuring impact framework	
Developed by	World business council for sustainable development
Purpose	To help organizations assessing their contribution to society and communicate it to investors and other stakeholder
Content	It thoroughly outlines a framework for businesses to measure their impact on development goals in the regions where they operate. The framework is laid out broadly to meet the needs of organizations across different sectors anywhere in the world over time, allowing a variety of businesses to make key decisions that affect social impact
Source	http://www.wbcsd.org/pages/edocument/edocumentdetails.aspx?id=205&nosearchcontextkey=true

Millennium development goal scan	
Developed by	Business in development and sustainalytics
Purpose	To assess organizations' contribution to the UN Millennium Development Goals and to demonstrate their role in achieving them
Content	It estimates your company's positive impact on the Millennium Development Goals, it estimates the number of people in developing countries benefitted by your company's activities (online tool)
Source	http://www.mdgscan.com/#page=Textpage&item=about_scan

Practical quality assurance system for small organizations	
Developed by	Charities evaluation services
Purpose	To help management running effectively and efficiently the organizations
Content	Is a work pack that convers 12 quality standards and promotes continuous improvement through self-assessment: (1) Planning for quality; (2) Governance; (3) Management; (4) User-centered service; (5) Staff and volunteers; (6) Training and development; (7) Managing money; (8) Managing resources; (9) Managing activities; (10) Networking and partnership; (11) Monitoring and evaluation; (12) Results
Source	http://www.ces-vol.org.uk/PQASSO/pqasso-the-basics

SOCIAL	
Developed by	ACCION
Purpose	This model measures the social impact of a microfinance institute (MFI)
Content	This is accomplished by forming a social performance assessment team to conduct audits by interviewing management, staff, board members, and clients; reviewing the strategic and business plans and minutes of board meetings; reviewing data from the MFI's client database; gathering data from external surveys or other sources to validate the MFI's database and searching secondary source data, such as national data, the MIX, market studies, etc.; creating a map of geographic coverage; and making branch visits. The result is a detailed social audit report for the institution and a social scorecard
Source	http://trasi.foundationcenter.org/record.php?SN=2

Social investment risk assessment	
Developed by	Hunter consulting LLC
Purpose	To let the leaders of social or human service agencies evaluate whether their clients are apt to benefit, as intended, from the programming and services their agency offers
Content	A "low risk" rating means that clients are likely to benefit as intended; conversely, a "high risk" rating means that the likelihood that clients will benefit is low. The SIRASA will immediately generate a Report to the organization once all thirty questions have been answered. This Report consists of a single score plus a paragraph discussing the organization's likely strengths and weaknesses with regard to program performance management
Source	http://www.dekhconsulting.com/

Social accounting and audit	
Developed by	Social audit network
Purpose	To help organizations assessing their contribution to society and communicate it to investors and other stakeholder
Content	It aims to collecting performance information and it focuses on a means of revealing the missing value that is being created (or destroyed) by that organization. There are 3 steps: (1) Getting ready; (2) Planning; (3) Accounting; (4) Reporting and audit
Source	http://www.socialauditnetwork.org.uk/getting-started/what-is-social-accounting-and-audit/

Third sector performance dashboard	
Developed by	Social firms UK
Purpose	To help organizations in monitoring and reporting on performance
Content	It provides a frame with typical key objectives and related typical measures for each of them
Source	http://www.socialfirmsuk.co.uk/resources/library/third-sector-performance-dashboard

Impact reporting and investment standard	
Developed by	Acumen Fund, B Lab, Rockefeller Foundation
Purpose	To assess social and environmental performance
Content	A series of indicators which guide organizations in reporting their social efforts
Source	http://iris.thegiin.org/

GIIRS	
Developed by	B Lab
Purpose	To measure social and environmental impact of companies and funds
Content	GIIRS (which stands for the Global Impact Investing Ratings System) is a comprehensive and transparent system for assessing the social and environmental impact of companies and funds with a ratings and analytics approach analogous to Morningstar investment rankings and Capital IQ financial analytics. It seeks to spark the impact investment movement by providing a tool that is intended to change investor behavior and unlock the potential of this new asset class
Source	http://giirs.org/

Social enterprise balanced scorecard	
Developed by	Social Enterprise London (SEL)
Purpose	To help organizations in assessing and communicating their social impact
Content	It's aimed at clarify and articulate organizations' strategic objectives and track performances through both qualitative and quantitative data. Through the creation of a strategic map an organization could create a visual representation of the critical elements of its strategy for both social and financial sides. The process then helps the organization to identify the key drivers or ways of achieving success from these social and financial perspectives by identifying what key stakeholders want from the organization, and what processes the organization needs to put in place internally for it to deliver these things
Source	http://www.sel.org.uk/Balanced-scorecard/

HIP (Human Impact + Profit) Scorecard	
Developed by	HIP Investor, Inc.
Purpose	To measure, manage, and communicate the goals and results of organizations sustainability efforts in one comprehensive, meaningful and informative presentation
Content	It measures five categories: health, wealth, earth, equality, and trust. HIP also assesses five management practices that drive sustainable, profitable growth: vision, measures, decision-making, accountability, and financial alignment. Organizations are analyzed using a combination of company interviews, primary research and third-party databases. The resulting HIP rating integrates 3 dimensions: human impact, profit, and management practices—and can be used as a tool inside organizations, to benchmark performance, to evaluate competitive position, and to communicate the level of impact to stakeholders across all sectors
Source	http://hipinvestor.com/for-companies/hip-scorecards/

Methodology for impact analysis and assessment	
Developed by	Investing for Good
Purpose	To examine an organization and its impact
Content	The three main areas covered are: 1. Mission Fulfillment; 2. Beneficiary Perspective; and 3. Wider Impact
Source	http://www.investingforgood.co.uk/publications/the-good-analyst/

Success measures data system	
Developed by	Neighbor works America
Purpose	It is a web-based tool which allows organizations to manage a participatory evaluation process efficiently and affordably. The accessible and flexible platform helps organizations capture a clear picture of benefits achieved by using combinations of off-the-shelf or customized data collection tools, collecting and tabulating results, and exporting data
Content	It foresees 5 phases: (1) plan; (2) design evaluation; (3) collect data; (4) analyze; (5) communicate
Source	http://www.successmeasures.org/data-system

Acumen Scorecard	
Developed by	Acumen Fund and McKinsey
Purpose	The AcumenSMS was developed to assist both for profit businesses, and not-for-profit organizations focus on actions that deliver both immediate results and improve an organizations long term competitive positioning in changing and dynamic marketplaces
Content	The AcumenSMS software helps leadership build tools and techniques to manage across five different perspectives: financial, internal business process, customers, learning & growth, and vision, governance and continuity
Source	http://www.acumensms.com/introduction.aspx

Charity assessment method of performance	
Developed by	Dutch charities test (nationale goede doelen test)
Purpose	The performance of charity's ADT are determined by effectiveness—What did we achieve?—And efficiency—how fast and in a cost-effective way?
Content	Effectiveness and efficiency can be measured on five distinct levels: 1. Impact on society: how is society is affected by the effect of the charity on their target group? 2. Impact on the public: in what way is the situation of the target group demonstrably improved by the output of the charity? 3. Output: what concrete results are produced by the core activities of the charity using the input factors (money, volunteers, etc.)? 4. Activities: how effective are the core activities of the charity? 5. Input: how effective and efficient are the activities related to the input factors such as fundraising and recruiting volunteers?'
Source	http://www.goededoelentest.nl/

Participatory Impact Assessment	
Developed by	Feinstein International Center
Purpose	Participatory Impact Assessment (PIA) applies the participatory methodology to the original corporational objectives in asking the critical questions "what difference are we making?"
Content	The framework does not aim to provide a rigid or detailed step by step formula, or set of tools to carry out project impact assessments, but describes an eight stage approach, and presents examples of tools which may be adapted to different contexts
Source	http://fic.tufts.edu/assets/PIA-guide_revised-2014-3.pdf

Star Social Firm	
Developed by	Social firms UK
Purpose	The Star Social Firm is a quality standard that is awarded to Social Firms that have proved the quality of their business and the employment they provide for severely disadvantaged people
Content	Organizations that want to apply for this requirement has to meet some criteria related to enterprise, employment and empowerment
Source	http://www.starsocialfirms.co.uk/

COSA Methodology	
Developed by	Sustainable commodity initiative
Purpose	It provides accurate measurement of recognized sustainability indicators along social, economic and environmental lines (farm sector)
Content	The COSA project will provide the first set of objective data and analyses on the social, economic and environmental costs and benefits of any sustainability efforts including those of the standards or certifications currently operating. The analysis and corresponding data set were also designed to serve a wide variety of analytic systems including: Relevance Tree Analysis; Cross Impact Analysis; Lifecycle Analysis; Emergy Analysis; and Ecological Footprinting
Source	http://www.sustainablecommodities.org/cosa/approach

Simple Social Quantitative Models

SOUL (Soft Outcomes Universal Learning) record	
Developed by	City College Norwich
Purpose	To measure soft outcomes and informal learning
Content	It specifically measures adults' progress in attitude, personal/interpersonal and practical skills and children and young peoples' progress against 'Every Child Matters' criteria
Source	www.soulrecord.org

Best Available Charitable Option (BACO)	
Developed by	Acumen fund
Purpose	To quantify the social impact of an investment
Content	Rather than seek an absolute standard for social return across an extremely diverse portfolio, it si aimed to quantify an investment's social impact and compare it to the universe of existing charitable options for that explicit social issue. Specifically, this tool helps inform investors where their philanthropic capital will be most effective—answering the question "For each dollar invested, how much social output will this generate over the life of the investment relative to the best available charitable option?"
Source	http://www.acumenfund.org/knowledge-center.html?document=56

Local Multiplier 3	
Developed by	New Economic Foundation (NEF)
Purpose	To assess the entity of money re-spent in the community, the local economic impact
Content	The measuring process starts with an analysis of the source of income and the ways it is spent and re-spent in the local area. It is based on the concept of "multiplier": money re-spent in the local economies means an higher multiplier effect because more income is generated. There are 5 general stages: (1) Determination of local area; (2) Identification of sources; (3) Determine how you spend your income into the local area; (4) Survey people or business you spend your money on to understand how they spend their incomes; (5) Collate all responses
Source	http://www.pluggingtheleaks.org/resources/plm_lm3.htm

Social Return On Investment—SROI	
Developed by	The roberts enterprise development funds
Purpose	To quantify social impact
Content	This is a six-steps method: (1) Identifying key stakeholder; (2) Mapping outcomes; (3) Evidencing outcomes and giving them value; (4) Establishing impact; (5) Calculating the SROI; (6) Reporting, using and embedding
Source	http://www.sroi-uk.org/home-uk

MicroRate	
Developed by	MicroRate
Purpose	To measure the level of social return from an investment in a microfinance institution
Content	The first component—social results—evaluates the MFI's capacity, efficiency, and consistency in achieving its social mission by considering depth and diversity of services; cost, efficiency, and sustainability; and institutional responsibility. The second component—social commitment—assesses the MFI's focus and the chances of potential deviation from the social mission by examining the MFI's mission, communication, management, strategic planning, monitoring, client protection, customer service, recruitment and training, and incentive system. After analyzing these two components, MicroRate arrives at a social rating grade
Source	http://www.microrate.com/mfis/social-rating

Movement Above the U.S. $1 a Day Threshold	
Developed by	Microcredit Summit Campaign
Purpose	To determine whether and where clients of microfinance institutions are leaving poverty, defined as moving from below US$1/day to above that threshold
Content	There are three prongs to this methodology: (1) analyzing existing data about a microcredit client's movement across US$1/day; (2) administering new surveys to establish baseline data for entering clients so their progress can be tracked over time; and (3) commissioning expert panels of top poverty researchers in various countries with high concentration of microfinance activities to ensure that accurate estimates of client's net exit from below U.S. $1/day is captured. The second item is a poverty scorecard of 10 questions that loan officers administer during loan applications and maintenance interviews with clients to measure the poverty level of their clients at entry and periodically over time
Source	http://www.microcreditsummit.org/movement_above_one_dollar_per_day/

Pulse—portfolio data management system	
Developed by	Acumen fund
Purpose	To allows the investor to track a consistent set of core quantitative financial, operational and social metrics for each portfolio company
Content	It creates and tracks customized metrics for individual companies and qualitatively rates company management using a standardized capabilities assessment of six areas: alignment with the investor's mission, financial sustainability, potential for scale, potential for social impact, management capability, and business model effectiveness
Source	http://www.acumenfund.org/investments/investment-performance/pulse.html

Expected return	
Developed by	Hewlett foundation
Purpose	To calculate the expected return of an investment
Content	It works multiplying (benefit in a perfect world x likelihood of success x philanthropy's contribution)/cost
Source	Maas, K., & Liket, K. (2011). Social Impact Measurement: Classification of Methods. In Environmental Management Accounting and Supply Chain Management (pp. 171–202). Springer, Netherlands

The FINCA client assessment tool	
Developed by	FINCA
Purpose	It is an open source tool in the form of a 40 min survey that measures internationally comparable variables of microfinance clients' social well-being
Content	The methodology utilizes a two stage cluster sampling approach to comprehensively survey clients regarding income sources and dependents, monthly household expenditures, daily per capita expenditures and poverty levels that collectively document expenditures on the six social metrics: household food security, health care, housing, education, empowerment, and social capital. Client responses are directly entered into PDA devices, which facilitate reliable data gathering and analysis
Typology of impact	Societal; Economic
Typology of model	Method
Source	http://www.kintera.org/site/c.6fIGIXMFJnJ0H/b.6088807/k.9066/FINCA_Client_Research_Tools.htm#.VD_aIfl_u-0

Social value metrics	
Developed by	Root capital
Purpose	It is a performance monitoring system that tracks the impact of loans
Content	It assesses economic (volume of sales, revenue, net assets, and the price premium a cooperative fetches for their product versus standard price); social (includes number of members, jobs created, amount of purchases from local rural producers, and price the cooperative pays local producers relative to the price a middleman would pay); and environment (includes total acres under organic certification, the number of trees planted in the past year, and the percentage of borrowers located in or around protected areas) impact of a loan. Questions are included in a standard loan application form
Source	http://svtgroup.net/wp-content/uploads/2011/09/SROI_approaches.pdf http://www.rootcapital.org/performance-reports

Social rating	
Developed by	M-CRIL
Purpose	To assess the use of microfinance resource
Content	Social rating contributes to greater transparency on what microfinance is achieving in terms of the double (indeed triple) bottom line. A Social Rating evaluates an MFI's performance in: Governance and Strategy, Monitoring Social goals, HR and Responsibility to staff, Client Protection, Depth of outreach, quality of services
Source	http://www.m-cril.com/SocialRating.aspx

Social performance indicators	
Developed by	CERISE
Purpose	It's a social audit tool for microfinance
Content	This is a social audit tool for microfinance institutions that takes the form of a questionnaire. It can be self-administered by the microfinance institute or used with an external reviewer that evaluates four dimensions: (1) outreach to the poor and excluded populations; (2) adaptation of products and services for target clients; (3) improvement in social and political capital; and (4) corporate social responsibility. The SPI tool is open access. In exchange for using the tool, users send their findings to CERISE along with comments on the tool. This user collaboration has led to an improved version of the SPI and a rich database with results of over 200 social audits
Source	http://www.cerise-microfinance.org/-impact-and-social-perfomance

Cost per impact	
Developed by	Center for Hight Impacts Philantropy—University of Pennsylvania
Purpose	To help a donor make decision based on an empirical definition of success for a given objective, which is linked to the costs required to achieve this success
Content	The cost per beneficiary is multiplied by the success rate
Source	http://www.impact.upenn.edu/images/uploads/UPenn_CHIP_CostPerImpact_Pathways_Dec08.pdf

Social footprint	
Developed by	Center for sustainable organizations
Purpose	To monitor and report organizations impact on people and society
Content	It measures the gap between resources people need and resources organizations decide to produce
Source	http://www.sustainableorganizations.org/the-social-footprint.html

Stakeholder value added	
Developed by	Leuphana Universität Lüneburg
Purpose	It represents a company's worth to shareholders in the absence of liabilities and capital costs
Content	It foresees four steps. In the first two steps, the return on stakeholder (RoSt) is calculated for the corporation in question and the reference corporation (e.g. market average). The RoSt represents the stakeholder's relative contribution to the value of the corporation. In the third step the RoSt of the reference corporation is subtracted from the RoSt of the corporation in view. In the final step this is multiplied by the corporation's stakeholder costs to obtain the stakeholder value added.'
Source	http://www.un.org/esa/sustdev/sdissues/technology/stakeholdervalue.pdf

Business ethic excellence model	
Developed by	European business ethics network (EBEN)—GR
Purpose	The implementation of the EBEN GR BEE Model can lead to an alternative approach for measuring Social Return on Investment using a semi-quantitative technique for assessing business ethics excellence performance. Weight factors will be assigned to the ten criteria of the Model, which will subsequently be used to measure SROI
Content	The Model contains ten criteria which are divided in three areas: standard corporate code, corporate governance and corporate social responsibility
Source	Antonaras, A., Iacovidou, M., & Memtsa, C. (2011). Measuring social return on investment using the EBEN GR Business Ethics Excellence Model. Verslo ir teisės aktualijos/Current Issues of Business and Law, 6(1), 69–89

24193459R00071

Made in the USA
Middletown, DE
17 September 2015